Jewish American Food Culture

Food Cultures in America
Ken Albala, General Editor

African American Food Culture
William Frank Mitchell

Asian American Food Culture
Jane E. Dusselier

Latino Food Culture
Zilkia Janer

Jewish American Food Culture
Jonathan Deutsch and Rachel D. Saks

Regional American Food Culture
Lucy M. Long

Jewish American
Food Culture

JONATHAN DEUTSCH AND RACHEL D. SAKS

Food Cultures in America
Ken Albala, General Editor

GREENWOOD PRESS
Westport, Connecticut • London

Library of Congress Cataloging-in-Publication Data

Deutsch, Jonathan, 1977–
    Jewish American food culture / Jonathan Deutsch and Rachel D. Saks.
        p. cm.—(Food cultures in America)
    Includes bibliographical references and index.
    ISBN 978–0–313–34319–3 (alk. paper)—ISBN 978–0–313–34127–4 (set :
    alk. paper)
    1. Food habits—United States.   2. Jews—United States—Social life and
customs.   3. Food in popular culture.   4. Jewish cookery.   I. Saks,
Rachel D.   II. Title.
    GT2853.U5D48   2008
    394.1'2—dc22   2007045393

British Library Cataloguing in Publication Data is available.

Library of Congress Catalog Card Number: 2007045393
ISBN: 978–0–313–34319–3 (vol.)
        978–0–313–34127–4 (set)

First published in 2008

Greenwood Press, 88 Post Road West, Westport, CT 06881
An imprint of Greenwood Publishing Group, Inc.
www.greenwood.com

Printed in the United States of America

∞™

The paper used in this book complies with the
Permanent Paper Standard issued by the National
Information Standards Organization (Z39.48–1984).

10   9   8   7   6   5   4   3   2   1

The publisher has done its best to make sure the instructions and/or recipes in this book
are correct. However, users should apply judgment and experience when preparing recipes,
especially parents and teachers working with young people. The publisher accepts no
responsibility for the outcome of any recipe included in this volume.

Contents

Series Foreword

If you think of iconic and quintessentially American foods, those with which we are most familiar, there are scarcely any truly native to North America. Our hot dogs are an adaptation of sausages from Frankfurt and Vienna; our hamburgers are another Germanic import reconfigured. Ketchup is an invention of Southeast Asia, although it is based on the tomato, which comes from South America. Pizza is a variant on a Neapolitan dish. Colas are derived from an African nut. Our beloved peanuts are a South American plant brought to Africa and from there to the U.S. South. Our french fries are an Andean tuber, cooked with a European technique. Even our quintessentially American apple pie is made from a fruit native to what is today Kazakhstan.

When I poll my students about their favorite foods at the start of every food class I teach, inevitably included are tacos, bagels, sushi, pasta, fried chicken—most of which can be found easily at fast food outlets a few blocks from campus. In a word, American food culture is, and always has been profoundly globally oriented. This, of course, has been the direct result of immigration, from the time of earliest settlement by Spanish, English, French and Dutch, of slaves brought by force from Africa, and later by Germans, Italians, Eastern Europeans, including Jews, and Asians, up until now with the newest immigrants from Latin America and elsewhere.

Although Americans have willingly adopted the foods of newcomers, we never became a "melting pot" for these various cultures. So-called ethnic cuisines naturally changed on foreign soil, adapting to new ingredients and popular taste—but at heart they remain clear and proud descendants of their respective countries. Their origins are also readily recognized by Americans;

we are all perfectly familiar with the repertoire of Mexican, Chinese, and Italian restaurants, and increasingly now Thai, Japanese, and Salvadoran, to name a few. Eating out at such restaurants is a hallmark of mainstream American culture, and despite the spontaneous or contrived fusion of culinary styles, each retains its unique identity.

This series is designed as an introduction to the major food cultures of the United States. Each volume delves deeply into the history and development of a distinct ethnic or regional cuisine. The volumes further explore these cuisines through their major ingredients, who is cooking and how at home, the structure of mealtime and daily rituals surrounding food, and the typical meals and how they are served, which can be dramatically different from popular versions. In addition, chapters cover eating out, holidays and special occasions, as well as the influence of religion, and the effect of the diet on health and nutrition. Recipes are interspersed throughout. Each volume offers valuable features including a timeline, glossary and index, making each a convenient reference work for research.

The importance of this series for our understanding of ourselves is severalfold. Food is so central to how we define ourselves, so in a sense this series will not only recount how recipes and foodways serve as distinct reminders of ethnic identity, binding families and communities together through shared experiences, but it also describes who we have all become, since each food culture has become an indispensable part of our collective identity as Americans.

Ken Albala
General Editor

Introduction: Jewish American Diversity

The challenge in writing a book about Jewish American food is that the diversity of Jewish Americans is consistent with the diversity of the United States. In writing about Jewish Americans are we discussing those who observe the Jewish dietary laws (kashrut)? Are we writing about those born into the Jewish faith, but who may not actively practice the religion? Are we discussing Arabic-speaking Jewish Americans who came from North Africa, speakers of contemporary Hebrew who came from Israel, or Jewish Americans who speak Russian and came to the United States from the former Soviet republics? Are we covering Jewish Americans who have a tradition of publicly embracing and celebrating their tradition or those who have been encouraged or conditioned to keep their identity low-key? Are we exploring an urban Hasidic community in Brooklyn, a multiethnic suburb of Los Angeles, or a rural town in North Dakota where there are only a handful of non-Christians?

The answer is a resounding "yes" to all. In this book we embrace the diversity of the American Jewish experience while seeking to find common denominators by which to explore the foods of daily routine, dining out, and holiday and life-cycle events.

For the purposes of this book Jewish Americans are those who self-identify as Jewish. They may or may not be religious. If religious they may be Reform, Reconstructionist, Conservative, Orthodox, Ultraorthodox, or another category. They may be culturally Jewish or culturally secular.

In table I.1 religion is on the vertical axis and cultural tradition on the horizontal. There are American Jews on the lower right quadrant who are both highly religious and highly traditional. On the subject of food, these

TABLE I.1
Religious Observance and Tradition Takes
Many Forms for American Jews

		Cultural Traditions	
		Low	High
Religion	Low	Non-Religious Non-Traditional	Non-Religious Traditional
	High	Religious Non-Traditional	Religious Traditional

Jewish Americans may frequently eat traditional Jewish food prepared under the strict observance of the Jewish dietary laws. In the upper left quadrant are Jewish Americans who identify as neither religious nor traditional. These Jewish Americans, Jewish by ancestry, may observe only major holidays, probably do not keep kosher, and may have a diet similar to that of any American in their region of the country. The lower left quadrant shows Jewish Americans who may be religious, attend synagogue regularly, and observe kosher laws, but adapt and embrace other aspects of mainstream American culture. These are Jewish Americans who, for example, may gather after work with friends at a kosher pizzeria. Finally, in the upper right quadrant there are Jewish Americans who are traditional but not religious. These Jewish Americans may observe Jewish holidays, speak Yiddish and/or Hebrew, and cook Jewish foods, but may not strictly observe kosher laws or other aspects of the religion. Such Jewish Americans may keep a kosher-style home but relax the rules further when dining out or traveling. Of course many Jewish Americans may not fit into any such categories or may bounce among them over the course of a lifetime. Like Americans in general, Jewish Americans have a diverse series of identities—cultural, ethnic, national, religious, occupational, and family.

JEWISH AMERICAN FOOD

Consistent with the diversity of American Jews, Jewish American food represents all of these traditions. In this book we try not to limit the explanations to the traditional, the religious, or the regional.

While Jews look to Israel as a religious and cultural homeland, for thousands of years Jews have led a Diasporic existence throughout the world.

Major areas of Jewish settlement include North Africa, the Middle East, the Mediterranean, Southern and Western Europe, Eastern Europe into Eurasia, and, of course, the United States, Canada, and parts of South America. A nation of immigrants, the United States has absorbed—and typically welcomed—Jews from all of these regions, just as they have non-Jews from these regions and from throughout the rest of the world.

American Jewish food, then, is as diverse as American Jews are. We may envision a Sabbath (Shabbat) dinner in the United States to be a boiled chicken, which is traditional in Ashkenazi (specifically Eastern European) tradition, but the same chicken may just as easily appear in Ethiopian Jewish American *doro* wat, a Moroccan Jewish American *tagine*, or a Persian Jewish American *fesenjan*. Similarly, a kosher or nonkosher weeknight meal for Jewish Americans may be an Israeli falafel with tabbouleh salad just as easily as it might be a Polish stuffed cabbage, Greek lamb with orzo, Italian spaghetti, or Chinese fried rice.

ABOUT THIS BOOK

In this book we celebrate the diversity of the Jewish American table by explaining the complexity of practice (for example, how a pulled pork sandwich can be lunch for one Jewish American and stomach-turning and forbidden even to touch to another) while seeking to explore common ground. We also acknowledge the vastness and rich complexity of our nation. Just as there is no single way Americans eat, there is no single way American Jews eat.

After a timeline, Chapter 1 provides a historical overview of the Jewish people throughout the world, ending with periods of immigration to the United States. Chapter 2 looks at major foods and ingredients in the American Jewish diet. Chapter 3 explores how the foods are cooked and who cooks them. Chapter 4 introduces typical everyday meals, and Chapter 5 considers the pleasures and challenges of dining out. The most in-depth chapters are 6 and 7, where holidays and other special occasions, and health and diet, especially the Jewish kosher laws, are explored. The book concludes with a number of resource suggestions for further study, a selected bibliography, and an index. Photos, line drawings and recipes complement the text.

Chronology

Circa 1800 B.C.E.	Abraham and descendents migrate from Mesopotamia (present-day Iraq) to Canaan (present-day Israel and parts of Lebanon). The Mesopotamian diet included grains, especially barley as a porridge, and coarse bread, along with onions, herbs, fresh and dried fruits, and small amounts of animal fat and dairy.
Circa 1300 B.C.E.	Settlement by additional Israelite tribes, including Jews from the Exodus from Egypt. The Bible tells of matzah (unleavened bread) and manna.
Circa 1000 B.C.E.	Jewish conquest of Jerusalem. Construction of first temple in Jerusalem under King Solomon. Diet at this time consists largely of coarse breads, grains, pulses (beans), wine, cheese, herbs, and meat for the rich.
586 B.C.E.	Destruction of the first temple by the Babylonians and expulsion of Jews from the region.
539 B.C.E.	Fall of Babylonian Empire and resettlement of Jerusalem by the Jews. Diet continues to be heavily agricultural, especially with renewed settlement.
519 B.C.E.	Rebuilding of the temple under Persian rule.

331 B.C.E.	Fall of Persian Empire to Alexander the Great.
312 B.C.E.	Division of Alexander's empire results in Syrian rule of Israel.
166 B.C.E.	Jewish rebellion against Syrians led by Judah Maccabee, made famous in the story of Hanukkah. Diet in this time period includes a large variety of cultivated fruits, beans, and nuts as well as nutritionally and culturally important wine, fresh cheese, olives and olive oil, and grains.
70 C.E.	First Jewish revolt, war against the Romans. Destruction of second temple by the Romans.
131	Second Jewish revolt fails. Jews are banned from Jerusalem by the Emperor Hadrian. Hadrian renames Judea "Palestine." Throughout their exile, Jews travel the region, mixing their food traditions with those of the majority population.
200	Recording of the Mishnah, the Jewish oral law.
450–700	Recording of the Talmud, Rabbinical commentary on Jewish law. Much commentary on kashrut (kosher law) is included.
Circa 630	Arabs conquer Jerusalem. Diet around this time remains primarily bread, fresh and dried fruit, olives, and greens with meat such as lamb, goat, and mutton for the rich.
900–1030	Muslim rule of Spain, where Jewish culture flourishes. Christian and Arab culinary traditions shape the foodways of Spanish Jews.
1099	Christian crusaders conquer Jerusalem; many Jews killed or expelled.
1290	Jews expelled from England by Edward I.
1492–1500	The Alhambra Decree: approximately 200,000 Jews are expelled from Spain, Portugal, and Germany, relocating to Poland, the Netherlands, Turkey, and the Middle East, including Palestine. Jewish food further evolves in this exile, picking up influences from the dominant cultures.

1517	Ottoman Turks conquer Palestine.
1542	German theologian Martin Luther fuels anti-Semitic sentiment in Europe with the publication of his tract, *On the Jews and Their Lies*.
1567	First yeshiva (Jewish university) founded in Poland.
1654	Portuguese assume control of Brazil from the Dutch. Jews living in Brazil travel to New Amsterdam (present-day New York).
1655	Jews readmitted to England by Oliver Cromwell.
1678	First Jewish cemetery in America established in Rhode Island.
1730	Shearith Israel Synagogue, America's first synagogue, built in Manhattan.
1740–1750	Influx of Jews into Palestine.
1775	Pope Pius VI issues edict to suppress Jewish religion.
1776	American Revolution allows for freedom of religion.
1789	French Revolution allows Jews to become French citizens.
1799	Napoleon at Acre declares Palestine a Jewish state but cannot enforce its establishment.
1831–1840	Egyptians conquer Palestine; Ottomans retreat.
1845	David Levy Yulee (D-Florida) is first Jew elected to U.S. Senate.
Mid-1800s	Emergence of Zionist movement, seeking to establish Jewish homeland in Palestine. Jewish biblical foods and the foods of Palestine become popular as Jews consider the idea of a Jewish cuisine in a Jewish homeland.
	Emergence of Conservative and Reform Judaism movements in Germany, and later, the United States. Much attention is given to adapting the Jewish laws—including kosher laws—to modern life.

1870	Rokeach, an early kosher food company, opens in Brooklyn, New York.
1871	Esther *Levy's Jewish Cookery Book*, the first American Jewish cookbook, is published in Philadelphia, Pennsylvania.
1875	Hebrew Union College founded in Cincinnati, Ohio.
1881–1920	Russian pogroms kill and expel thousands of Jews from Russia and Ukraine. Many immigrate to the United States and Palestine.
1882	Yiddish theater opens in New York City.
1886	Founding of Jewish Theological Seminary in New York City.
1888	Katz's Delicatessen founded in New York City.
	Manischewitz, which will later become America's largest kosher food producer, opens its first plant in Cincinnati, Ohio.
1897	The Yiddish-language *Jewish Daily Forward* newspaper is founded in New York City.
1901	The *Settlement House Cookbook* is published as a fundraiser for the Jewish Settlement House in Milwaukee, Wisconsin.
1903	Oscar Straus is appointed U.S. Secretary of Labor, the first Jew to hold a Cabinet position.
1905	Hebrew National Foods, famous for its hot dogs, begins production in New York City.
1911	Crisco shortening is introduced to the market.
1914	Russ & Daughters appetizing store (a Jewish store specializing in preserved fish and dairy) opens in New York.
	The Neighborhood Cookbook by the Council of Jewish Women is published in Portland, Oregon.
1915	Founding of Yeshiva University in New York City.

1916	President Woodrow Wilson appoints the first Jewish member of the U.S. Supreme Court, Louis Brandeis.
	Nathan's Hot Dogs opens in Coney Island, Brooklyn, New York. First Fourth of July hotdog eating contest purportedly occurs.
1917	The British issue the Balfour declaration for "the establishment in Palestine of a national home for the Jewish people."
1919	*The International Jewish Cookbook* by Florence Kreisler Greenbaum is published in New York.
1933	Adolf Hitler comes to power in Germany. Already known as an anti-Semite, he prompts another wave of immigration to the United States, Palestine, and elsewhere.
1935	Coca Cola is certified kosher by Atlanta Rabbi Tobias Geffen.
1938–1945	The Holocaust (*ha shoah*) occurs in Europe; six million Jews are killed.
1945	Bess Myerson becomes first Jewish Miss America.
1945–1949	Post-war Jewish refugees struggle to immigrate to the United States, Palestine, and elsewhere.
1947	The United Nations approves the establishment of a Jewish state in Palestine.
1948	The state of Israel declares itself an independent nation and joins the United Nations.
	Arab-Israeli war (also called Israel War of Independence) takes place in response to establishment of the state of Israel.
1957	United States has the world's largest Jewish population.
1958	Temple Synagogue in Atlanta, Georgia is bombed by anti-Semites.
1972	Hebrew Union College ordains America's first woman rabbi.

1979–1991	Rescue of Ethiopian Jews to Israel; some subsequent immigration to the United States.
1990	Following fall of the Berlin wall Soviet Jews allowed to leave the Soviet Union, prompting wave of immigration to Israel, the United States, and elsewhere.
	Diane Feinstein (D-California) and Barbara Boxer (D-California) are first Jewish women elected to U.S. Senate.
1993	Ruth Bader Ginsburg is first Jewish woman appointed to U.S. Supreme Court.
	ConAgra acquires Hebrew National Foods.
2000	Senator Joseph Lieberman (D-Connecticut) is first Jewish candidate for national office (vice president) by a major party.
2001	First Annual Pickle Day celebrated in New York City's Lower East Side (New York Food Museum).
2007	Jewish American Food and Culture are featured in the Forshpeis! exhibit at the National Museum of American Jewish History in Philadelphia.

1

Historical Overview

Jews have a history that spans thousands of years, from biblical times. In this chapter we explore the history of the Jewish people with special attention given to providing context that will be useful in later chapters, specifically the history of Jewish people in the United States and the prominent and dynamic role of food and diet in Jewish history. The chapter begins with a historical exploration of the biblical period, continues through the Diaspora, and ends with major periods of Jewish immigration to the United States.

BIBLICAL HISTORY

Historians, archaeologists, and Bible scholars and critics often debate the early history of the Jews. Those who hold the Bible (the Jewish Bible, which is what will be referred to here as the Bible, is sometimes referred to as the Old Testament by non-Jews) to be a historical and truthful book only need to look as far as its pages to find the history of the Jews. Other scholars look deeper into the biblical period of history and use the Bible only as a guide or a possible social commentary, not a work of fact or history. Although biblical criticism and scholarship is a much debated issue today, especially among observant Jews, the focus here will be on history and archaeology and some biblical criticisms that view the Bible as a historically inconsistent and flawed yet telling text of the Jewish people.

Source Theory, also known as the Documentary Hypothesis, suggests that the Torah (the first five books of the Bible) was composed separately by four authors at different time periods with different social and political interests and was later combined and seamed together by an unknown redactor. The Documentary Hypothesis suggests that each of the sections of the Torah was written at some point during the period of the monarchies of Judea and Israel, between 900 and 400 B.C.E. Theorists believe that much of the text of the Bible was passed down orally from one generation to another and that some parts of the Bible are the telling of the same events from several different perspectives.

Despite the possibility that the Bible may not have been written by God, or that parts may have been written later than the lives of those who were supposed to have written them, archaeologists and historians have found many artifacts and documents and have done scientific tests to confirm many of the things mentioned in the Bible. Although the specifics of the stories surely cannot be verified, for our purposes here, the item of importance is that many of the places, foods, and ways of life that are described in the Bible are thought to be historically accurate.

FOOD

One thing that is clear is that food has always played an important role in Jewish history. The first sin of the Bible involves a piece of fruit—the story of Eve being tempted to eat what is commonly referred to as an apple, but probably was a pomegranate, from the Tree of Knowledge by the serpent. In a later story Jacob and Esau fight about their birthright over a pot of lentils. The book Song of Songs, which is a love poem, includes food as a part of its metaphoric images of the woman's body in the poem, and figs are mentioned in the Bible as a sign for fertility.

The history of Israel before the Exodus from Egypt is presented in the Bible as a family history of a group of people whose story includes constant interaction with God. Hospitality is known to have been one of the most important values for the people. This ties in closely with food, since guests and strangers were always given large portions of food. The first meal described in the Bible is an impromptu feast that Abraham gave angels. Sarah made bread or cakes and Abraham cooked a calf. Although historians would argue that there is no way to say whether or not this happened, or even whether or not Abraham and Sarah even existed, one can learn from this that the staples the people had at this time included bread (grain of some sort) and domesticated cattle. Archaeologists know from analyzing texts from this period that slaughtering a calf was a sign of great wealth.

From other archaeological excavations scholars have found remnants of different fruits from this period, including figs, grapes, and pomegranates. Also, remnants of wheat, barley, and other grains have been found. Although it is safe to say that the Jews of this period ate these foods, it is not possible to tell in what quantities they ate them or how they prepared them.

Pomegranates. © J. Susan Cole Stone.

The Biblical Patriarchal period ended when the Jews were said to have settled in Egypt. Joseph, an Israelite who was said to have spent time as a senior aid to the Pharaoh, detailed a hierarchy of food providers, each responsible for a different branch of the royal kitchen. The Egyptians were the first to discover fermentation and develop a process for baked leavened bread, and they had a variety of vegetables, fruits, beer, and bread as well as meat cattle, pigs, ducks, and geese. The also ate a variety of fish. Following their time in Egypt the Israelites were said to have left Egypt on an extremely long journey for what is present-day Israel. Before leaving, the Bible recounts that they rushed to make unleavened bread (matzah) to bring with them.

While wandering the desert, food was scarce and people began to complain, saying that they missed the rich supply of meat, fish, cucumbers, melons, leeks, onions, and garlic that they had in Egypt. God then provided manna; however, the people were not satisfied: "Now our gullets are shriveled. There is nothing at all! Nothing but this manna to look to! Now the manna was like coriander seed. . . . The people would go about and gather it, grind it between millstones or pound it into a mortar, boil it in a pot, and make it into cakes. It tasted like rich cream. When the dew fell on the camp at night, the manna would fall upon it" (Numbers 11:7–9). Also, there are times in which the Bible describes God providing a multitude of quails for the people.

Food is discussed a great deal during the time that the Israelites were wandering in the desert. In Deuteronomy there are seven basic agricultural products mentioned: wheat, barley, figs, grapes, olives, pomegranates, and honey. The Bible also mentions three staple products: corn (not maize, which is a product of the Americas, but rather a grain of some sort), wine, and oil (probably olive oil; rendered animal fat was also available), which, taken together, could have provided basic nutrients for a subsistence diet. Dough would have been baked directly on the sand or on heated stones covered with glowing ashes.

As the Israelites were still wandering the desert, there is a long set of commandments from God that detail for them how to perform sacrifices. The people were to make burnt offerings of cattle, birds, goats, and the like. The offering was meant to be from the best of the herd, and the animal would be slaughtered and then laid in sections upon the altar. People could also make offerings of flour or unleavened cakes with oil mixed in, or an offering of first fruits. All of the sacrifices must have had salt on them. There are specific instructions to the priests for how to give a sin offering (a bull) and to the people for their sin offering (a female goat or sheep). Since the destruction of the Temple in Jerusalem there are no longer Jewish priests or animal sacrifices, but these were important aspects of the religion historically.

While wandering the desert the people were also given a complex set of laws about what was acceptable for the Israelites to eat and what was not acceptable for them to eat. Many scholars believe that these laws were given as a way for the Israelites to differentiate themselves from their neighbors, particularly the Philistines. The Israelites were told that they would be allowed to eat any animal with cleft hooves that chews its cud, any fish with fins and scales, and any bird that is not a bird of prey. They were forbidden to eat most insects, animals with paws, reptiles, and rodents (Numbers 11). Although there is not a full explanation here of these laws (called the laws of kashrut), the rabbis and other future generations expounded upon them and formed them into a set of dietary guidelines that observant Jews follow today.

Some scholars believe that the laws of kashrut were essentially early public health measures, pointing out potentially hazardous foods to avoid. Others attribute the rules' origins as related to conceptions of holiness and the world's order in the Israelite worldview: things out of place, such as a sea creature that does not swim (a clam for example) became unkosher or *treyf*, which means that it is forbidden to eat the food.

The Israelites were said to have conquered the land of Canaan (present-day Israel) and then to have split up geographically by tribes. There was a period in which judges ruled the Israelites, and both then and afterward when the country was ruled by kings, there were a series of prophets who were the moral conscience of the people. The traditional preaching place for prophets was in the market. In Ezekiel God punishes the people for their poor behavior by telling Ezekiel to make a foul bread out of beans and grains and to bake a barley cake atop human excrement. When Ezekiel prophesies the fate of sinful Jerusalem he drives his message home by describing the methods of making a soup: "Thus said the Lord God: set on a pot, set it on, and also pour water into it. Gather the pieces thereof into it, even every good piece, the thigh, and the shoulder. Fill it with choice bones" (Ezekiel 25:3–6)—soup is made with the best parts, which symbolizes the best parts of Israeli society.

After the judges came a period in which kings ruled the Israelites, first in a short period of a monarchy that united all of the tribes, and then in a much longer period of a divided monarchy. The people were settled at this point and could begin to plant and harvest their own foods.

In the Middle Eastern diet, bread, probably a coarse wheat flatbread, not dissimilar to whole wheat pita, was the primary staple. The people developed an agricultural economy mainly based on cereal growing (wheat and barley were common grains in the Middle East). Barley had been the most important staple grain until the introduction of husked wheat around 4000 B.C.E.

Pulses or legumes were the next most important thing to bread: lentils, beans, and peas, which could be made into a potage (a thick soup) were often eaten with bread to form a complete protein, and, with the addition of vegetable and animal fats, scraps of meat, fish, fruit, and vegetables such as greens, the basis of a good diet. Archaeologists have found remnants of a wild ancestor of the fava bean, and also of peas and chickpeas. Cultivated vegetables played a minor role in the diet; however, people at this time did have onions and foraged for a wide variety of edible greens. Olives and grapes were important, but the olives were used mainly for oil and the grapes mainly for wine, rather than for table food.

The majority of people lived on a diet of coarse barley bread, roasted green wheat, fresh and roasted young lentils, butter, vegetables, and fruits (dried figs, dates, carob), supplemented by sheep's milk products and small amounts of honey, which was the only available sweetener. Meat, usually goat or sheep, was rarely eaten and was consumed at festive meals or tribal gatherings; the wealthy commonly had roasted lamb or boiled beef. Cooking pots were made of earthenware and held on clay stands built in a horseshoe shape.

MISHNAIC AND TALMUDIC ERAS

Solomon, the second king of the united monarchy of Israel, was said to have built the first Temple for the Jewish people in the tenth century B.C.E. The building of this Temple signified that the Israelites were now settled people who no longer had to live nomadic lives, although they had not had to live nomadic lives for quite some time. The building of the Temple really symbolized the first attempt to give Israel a center, both for worship and culture. This Temple was destroyed in 586 B.C.E. by the Babylonians and was rebuilt 70 years later in 516 B.C.E. This second Temple was then destroyed in 70 C.E. by the Romans, and the Jews were exiled from Jerusalem. There were two major Jewish communities after the destruction of the second Temple: in Babylonia (present-day Iraq, where many Jews were already settled because of the first destruction) and in Palestine (not Jerusalem, but many small villages in the Galilee).

Strangely enough, the expulsion did not bring about the destruction of the Jewish culture. On the contrary, being stateless forced the Jews to look at their past history, codify their holy writing, and start recording and explaining their oral traditions. Religious and civil laws were collected in a group of six books known as the Mishnah, compiled by 200 C.E. Rabbis and scholars met and discussed how to interpret the Bible and what that should mean for the everyday life of the exiled Jews. They debated how to stay traditional yet still adapt to their new life situation and covered topics ranging from holiday observance to agricultural practices to, of course, cooking and eating.

Soon after the Mishnah was finished, the rabbis of both the Babylonian and Palestinian communities began to compile an even more thorough examination of the laws and way of life of the Jewish people by composing the Talmud. Each community recorded the oral debates and discussions of what was written in the Mishnah just a few hundred years before. The rabbis would start their discussion based on one discussion in the Mishnah and would branch out into many different topics, sometimes going on for many pages. Although the Babylonian Talmud is the tome that is most widely used and commented upon, there is also a Palestinian Talmud, and both books are an interesting window into the lives of the Jews at this time. Observant Jews believe that the oral law (Mishnah and Talmud) are also words of God that were simply written down at a later point. Therefore, the discussions in the Talmud are considered legally binding.

The Exile created a new type of social order, which gave an opportunity for a new class of merchants to establish themselves and allowed the Babylonian community to flourish. When the Jews arrived in Babylon they found an already thriving community. Babylonians had a highly developed culture and an agricultural tradition that specialized in gardening and raising vegetables. Fish and other meats were commonly available, and Jews were introduced to new spices and more advanced methods of agriculture.

An important part of the narration of the Mishnah involves food, including information on dietary laws and eating and cooking practices. There was a clear division between rich and poor that was set forth in the Mishnah. The rabbis actually wrote that the minimal weekly alimony a divorcee should expect included about 4.4 liters of wheat, 1.25 liters of beans, .25 liters of oil, and 2.2 liters of dried figs (Ketubot 5:8). These foods, including wild leaves and vegetables that people may have collected, seem to have been the subsistence diet of the poor.

The poor also ate bread at every meal (the Mishnah demanded this), which was taken with salt or even a relish of olives and onions. Bitter wild leaves such as horseradish, chicory, or dandelion were also a popular accompaniment to the bread. The bread itself was made mainly from one of the major grains of the area: hard wheat, spelt, rice, or barley. Wheat replaced barley at this time as the most commonly used cereal; barley came to be considered a poor person's food. Although special breads made with fine ground flour were made for special occasions, the poor generally ate coarse and unrefined breads.

Common fruits and vegetables for the poor included cabbage, turnips, co-locasia (like a potato and used similarly), radishes, onions, legumes, melons, and cucumbers. Cabbage in particular was viewed as healing and nourishing. There were distinctions made by the rabbis between garlic and leek, which were viewed as necessities, and radishes and beets, which unless cooked properly, were thought to be deadly.

The wealthy community in Babylonia ate very differently from the poor community. They had houses that were organized around courts in which people did a lot of their cooking and drying of fruits. The stoves and cooking ranges were portable and made from clay. The portable ovens were beehive-shaped clay pots with an opening at the top. Pita was baked by sticking the thinly rolled dough on the walls and removing them once they were slightly charred in a method similar to cooking *na'an*, an Indian flatbread baked in a tandoor oven. The most widely used material for cooking equipment was clay, but there was also wood, glass, stone, and metal available in varying qualities.

Next in importance to bread and grain were pulses. Widely eaten by both the wealthy and the poor, bean dishes were richer in protein than cereals and were relatively inexpensive. However, in order for the beans to be fully nutritionally effective they had to be eaten in a diet that included grain of some kind. In addition to chickpeas, lentils, and broadbeans, there were cow-peas, lupines, grass peas, and vetch. Beans and lentils were either eaten raw, roasted, or cooked, both fresh and dry. Dry beans were broken into rough pieces and cooked in porridge-like dishes.

Vegetables were increasingly important during this period. The Mishnah details a process of pickling, in which different vegetables were combined and placed in a salt water mixture. Heavy stones were placed on top of the vegetables to prevent air from reaching them and the people could then enjoy pickled fruits and vegetables, including melons, zucchini, cucumbers, capers, and artichokes.

The rabbis of the Mishnah mention many fruits and vegetables in their various debates, including apples, apricots, melons, watermelons, pears, peaches, pomegranates, mulberries, quinces, carobs, and lemons. They also detail many spices (some of which are difficult to identify today) including coriander, dill, cumin, fennel, anise, caraway, celery, thyme, marjoram, sage, mint, nutmeg, ginger, cinnamon, black pepper, and mustard. Most families ate their bread with vegetables either as a sandwich or in the form of a stew. During the winter people gathered wild herbs, artichoke, ginger, celery, and watercress. Vegetables and fruits were eaten fresh, dried, and preserved, or they were cooked, stewed, and fried.

Although milk was not a regular part of the Jewish people's diet at this time, cheese is frequently mentioned in the Talmud. Also, it is possible to tell from archaeological evidence that people did not eat much red meat; they mostly ate poultry and fish for animal protein. When they did eat red meat they ate chiefly beef and lamb. Meat and chicken were primarily eaten on Shabbat, a tradition that continues to this day for many Jews.

Fish was quite popular and was eaten pickled, boiled, broiled, and cooked in milk, mixed with eggs and fried, or enjoyed with an egg on top. Also, sauces were made from fermented fish that were used as a condiment—there was even an entire fish course during Shabbat dinner during which a fish pie was eaten.

Palestinian food and Babylonian food, from the two major Jewish Diasporic communities of the time, were somewhat different from one another. Palestine had common Mediterranean foods of the time, such as wheat, wine, and olive oil, while sesame oil and beer were popular in Babylonia. The Palestinian Jewish community ate fewer grains and larger amounts of boiled beans and vegetables, and lentils were popular.

MIDDLE AGES

The Babylonian and Palestinian Talmuds were completed around the time of the beginning of the Middle Ages. At this point, Jews were spread out all over the Middle East, Eastern Europe, and Western Europe. This is the time when historians begin to classify Jews as either Ashkenazi (eastern, living mostly in Eastern Europe) or Sephardi (western, living throughout the Mediterranean, Iberia, North Africa, and the Middle East). Jewish communities existed outside of Israel since the reign of King Solomon. The Bible hints at the existence of trade with Spain and North Africa, and the Mishnah mentions both Italy and Spain. These communities included Jewish Palestinian émigrés, converts, and others. After the destruction of the two Temples these communities only grew further.

There are other Middle Eastern Jewish communities that were nomadic well into the sixth century and eventually settled into desert communities in places like Yemen. Most notable of the Sephardi communities is the medieval Spanish Jewish population that thrived and was a cultural center until the Jews were expelled in 1492.

Sephardi

Sephardi Jews share the fact that they primarily lived in countries that were at one time or another under the influence of Islam, a religion that shares many things with Judaism. Both are monotheistic religions that sprang from a Middle Eastern nomadic pastoral culture. Islam began to spread through Europe and the Middle East in the seventh century, and although the Jews in the Middle East were not accepted by the Muslims, they were tolerated because they posed no significant political or military threat. Although the differentiation of Sephardi and Ashkenazi did not come about until after the expulsion of the Jews from Spain in 1492, the different food pathways that led to this differentiation can already be seen in the early Middle Ages.

Because of the Ashkenazi-centric current Jewish population in the world there is scarce literature on Sephardi communities of the Middle Ages, especially on food. However, some things are known. Jews in the Islamic world were often very poor; however, there were some Jews who were quite wealthy. Bread was a staple food and was supplemented with spices, cheese, oil, legumes, and fruit. Yemeni and other Middle Eastern Jews used wheat for their breads and ate them with a clarified butter similar to Indian ghee. Pitas were eaten at breakfast with a paste made from soaked fenugreek seeds. In medieval Egypt bread was eaten with onions or garlic and thyme, radishes, or other herbs. The lower classes ate more fruit and fish than meat; however, when meat was eaten it was usually mutton, goat, lamb, or kid.

In North Africa there were more vegetables available, and they were used imaginatively in a variety of cooked and fresh salads and in countless crustless pies, which were composed by combining vegetables, meat, and eggs and baking them, almost like a quiche filling. Also in North Africa, Jews commonly distilled alcoholic drinks made from figs and dates.

The Spanish medieval Jewish community had perhaps the most varied cuisine of any medieval Sephardi community. One complicated recipe that may have originated from this community was a rich sweet made from layers of almond paste flavored with orange flower water, thin egg noodles cooked in boiling syrup, and lemon cut into thin slices and then baked until set. Little pies known as *burekas* were also popular. They were small pastries that contained sweet, savory, milk, and meat fillings, similar to empanadas.

Ashkenazi

The origins of the Jewish communities in Central and Eastern Europe are a bit unclear. Although there was probably a community of Jewish merchants that were established during the Roman Empire, the Jews only started moving into Eastern Europe to escape the Crusaders, who were killing anyone who was not Christian. Life in Christian Europe was certainly not easy for the Jews. They were thought of as Christ-killers and were ostracized in every way possible from the greater community. The primary occupation for Jews during this time was money lending; however, they were never fully stable in one place because any unrest often resulted in the Jews being kicked out of a certain community.

Although Jews were not accepted into the communities, it was during the Middle Ages that Jewish cuisine truly began to take the shape of the cuisine of whatever community they were a part of. The Jewish foods of Italy, Greece, and France had a great deal in common. For example, Italian recipes for pies, tortes, cakes, and vermicelli noodles became popular with the Jews of Italy and then traveled elsewhere. Meat pies and other cakes and pies filled with cheese or fruit were also popular at this time. Jews were taking many cues from Italian culture, specifically making vermicelli, and tortelli, which is probably where the modern noodle dishes of kugel and kreplach (a stuffed noodle similar to tortellini or ravioli) can find their origins. Jewish communities in Italy, Greece, and some of France are all considered to be Sephardi.

Although there were many similarities between Jewish and Italian, German, and French foods, certain vegetables such as beets and eggplants were rarely consumed by the greater population but were eaten in great numbers by the Jews because they were cheap and nutritious, reminding us of the low place of Jews in Christian society. One popular Jewish Italian dish was *carciofi alla guidia*, which are young artichokes fried in oil. Some rabbinic sources describe something called *floden*, which was a pastry of two layers of dough filled with cheese.

Italian, French, and German Jews ate poultry and game, stews, sheep, dove, goose, capons, ducks, pheasants, quail, duck, and smoked beef. They used a great deal of nutmeg and consumed vegetables, salted cheese, meat pies, baked meat, lentils, peas, beans, salted and cold meats, chicory, spinach, cabbage, lettuce, parsley, grapes, figs, raisins, almonds, pistachio nuts, melons, and soft, hard-boiled, and fried eggs. Fish was generally dried, smoked, salted, or pickled, and every Jewish community made different kinds of *cholent* (a slowly baked Sabbath stew of meat, beans and potatoes or barley) with different kinds of beans and meats depending on the area.

In France and Germany Jews ate beef pickled with vinegar and garlic, roast meat, salt beef, poultry, spiced meat, eggs fried in honey, different cakes, baked apples, cinnamon sticks, and biscuits. In Germany specifically pancakes were made with eggs, and omelets were popular. Omelets were sometimes filled with raisins, fish or minced meat, or cheese.

The poorest of the poor in Western Europe ate dark bread made with rye or barley, some cheese, or a bowl of curds for a meal. Poor German Jews ate meat, soup, fish, bread, vegetables, and fruit for dessert, while wealthier German Jews could afford meat, sausages, cabbages, lentils, rye bread, and beer. On Shabbat they ate freshwater fish such as trout and pike with mustard and horseradish, a predecessor to the modern Jewish Shabbat and holiday staple of gefilte fish with horseradish.

French Jews ate bread, coarse soups, gruel, cheese, and vegetables such as cabbages, onions, and leeks. On Shabbat they ate herring, salmon, and carp. They ate small fried fish, or fish served in a jelly or with different sauces.

ENLIGHTENMENT

After the Middle Ages and after the Jews were expelled from numerous European countries, the Jews along with the rest of the world entered the modern era. The beginnings of industrialization, the advent of the printing press, and many other factors contributed to both Jewish and secular communities experiencing drastic changes. This was the period of the emancipation movement all over Europe, freeing the Jews from some discriminatory rules, followed by the Jewish Enlightenment. In large numbers Jews began to seek integration into the cultural, economic, and political life of modern society, and they met extreme forms of resistance and a new type of anti-Semitism.

For European countries the beginning of the modern age is marked by the transition from the feudal era to the formation of centralized or absolute states. While some Jews became court Jews and were accepted by the monarchs because of their utility, most were still despised and had very few privileges. People began to see that if the Jews were granted equal opportunity and perhaps dignity then they could prove to be resourceful, loyal subjects.

The process of legal emancipation of the Jews, however, was ambiguous. The granting of citizenship did not necessarily signify a basic or widespread change in attitudes toward the Jews. In places like France Jews were told that they could be citizens but that their religion could in no way interfere with the obligations of their citizenship. Emancipation required that the all citizens completely integrate themselves into the culture of the nation. Because the Jews possess distinct cultural and national aspirations of their own, they were fundamentally incompatible with the modern states that had granted them emancipation. Jews who were not able to integrate themselves into enlightened European society experience a new kind of politically sanctioned anti-Semitism.

In sixteenth-century Europe a trend called Enlightenment began, in which philosophers and scholars held that the ultimate truth was reason (as opposed to religion). Many Jews who were newly emancipated and able to now take their place in secular society adopted these philosophical ideas and assimilated, leaving their religious life behind for the scholarly pursuit of truth.

Reason was considered to be a universal bond between men, which allowed for the liberal and democratic values that would eventually allow non-Jews to embrace Jews as fellow human beings.

As can be expected, there was a backlash to Jewish Enlightenment in the religious community. Hasidism, a movement of popular mysticism, emerged as the keeper of the Jewish tradition. They were quick and forceful in their warnings about the dangers of Enlightenment. Though many in this period attempted to be both Jews of the Enlightenment and Jews of tradition, they were ultimately rejected by the Jewish community.

For the more eastern European communities such as Poland and Russia, modern Jewish history began with the partitions of Poland in 1772 and with the incorporation of large numbers of Jews into Russia and other communities. The tsars responded to the huge numbers of Jews by restricting them to certain areas, known as the Pale of Settlement. The tsars attempted to undermine the Jewish way of life and to restructure their communal and social patterns by conscripting boys into the army and forcing assimilation. However, demographically, the Jews of Russia and Poland overall were confined to such few and small areas and were so heavily concentrated that there was little possibility for cultural or social assimilation.

Because of this ghettoizing, Eastern European Jews developed their own way of life. Religious denominationalism that was happening elsewhere did not happen in Eastern Europe. Places for intense Jewish study, called yeshivot, were developed, and the Jews spoke their own language, Yiddish. Jews settled in shtetls, which were small, confined, and crowded religious Jewish communities. There was one rabbi for each community who helped the Jews make all decisions concerning their way of life. Jews living in shtetls were not bothered much by the tsars or other government officials, at least until the pogroms beginning in 1880, in which the government of the various countries of Eastern Europe sanctioned the destruction of Jews and of their communities.

The food of Jews in Poland, Russia, Germany, and other Eastern European countries from the 1700s to the 1900s was relatively similar and was heavily influenced by the foods of the surrounding cultures. It was the woman's job to cook and serve food, and one of the most common preparations of food was to make it sweet and sour, like sauerbraten. A good deal is known about how the poor of Eastern Europe ate, especially since the majority of Jews at this time were poor. They ate mainly black bread, gruels, cheap vegetables, and herring. Russians mainly ate buckwheat groats (kasha), beets, cucumbers, and fresh or salt fish, and Polish Jews also ate bread from millet, rice, buckwheat, and peas, in addition to carrots, cucumbers, and radishes and coarse soups and gruels. Oil and goose or chicken fat were the main cooking mediums.

Breakfast usually consisted of bread with raw onion, radish, or turnip and a piece of brown bread rubbed with chicken or goose fat (schmaltz) and smeared with garlic. For more wealthy Jews the meal my have also included salt herring and smoked sausage and tea, fruit jellies dissolved in hot water, or coffee. For breakfast and lunch during the week people generally did not eat meat and instead ate mostly noodles, potatoes, bread, barley, buckwheat, and corn. Barley, buckwheat and other grains were used to make gruels and soups that were quite common.

Bread made from coarse rye flour was the most significant part of the diet in the nineteenth century. Bagels and other rolls were also widely eaten. People made their own noodles with noodle boards, and these noodles were used in a multitude of dishes.

From the mid-nineteenth century on, potatoes, a tuber of American origin, were a new staple in the diet, and the reliance on grain decreased. Potatoes were eaten two or three times a day and were enjoyed in a multitude of ways. They could be cooked with onions and pepper, baked in their skins and cooled, or eaten with raw shredded onions. They were also grated and made into pancakes (latkes), or mashed with chicken fat, plainly boiled, eaten with cabbage, carrots, and other vegetables as a treat, and on Shabbat served in a warm pudding. In Lithuania they grated potatoes and added flour made from buckwheat to make buns that were eaten plain or hot with sour cream and butter. Milk, sour cream, and cream were often used to supplement potato dishes.

Except for carrots, beets, onions, radish, garlic, and foraged greens, fresh vegetables were rarely eaten, but pickled vegetables were common. Pickled vegetables were extremely common because there was little opportunity for agriculture in the cold Eastern European climates. Jews sometimes ate a meal of very sour pickled cucumbers with bread. When in season markets had potatoes, beets, cabbages, carrots, green peas, berries, cucumbers, radishes, spring onions, and also, apples, pears, and cherries.

Beets were used to make a beet soup called borscht that is either made with meat and eaten hot or with vegetables and sour cream and eaten cold. Cabbage was also used to make different types of sauerkraut, and shav, a cold soup, was made with sorrel leaves, lemon juice, and sour cream. These foods were often made sour to counterbalance the dull taste of potatoes and black bread.

Meat was rarely served but was preferred over other foods. Liver was used extensively and was mainly chopped but was also served with onions or cooked in a sweet and sour sauce. Cow, ox, and calf feet were used to make soups, and the spleen was hollowed and stuffed with bread crumbs and then stewed with onions and pepper. Puddings were made from cow stomach and lung was used either as a stuffing for dumplings or pastries or served with noodles. Brains were special because of their soft and succulent texture; they were considered good for improving one's mind.

People ate poultry more often than beef, especially because many households kept chickens for their eggs. Some women even specialized in fattening chickens and geese. Goose meat was used in a similar way to pork fat and meat; the legs and thighs were brined and smoked like hams, the fat breast meat used to make pastrami (brined, coated with spices, hot smoked, and used in a way similar to bacon), and other meat was used in making sausages. Also, schmaltz, or goose or chicken fat, was very common.

Although people did not eat meat regularly, fish was a mainstay in the Eastern European diet. Salted herring was common and a lifesaver. It was cheap, long-lasting, nourishing, and a good source of protein. Herring was also used to make gefilte fish, a ground fish cake that was cooked in broth and combined with onions, garlic, and spices. Sometimes fish was cooked in a brown sauce or smoked and enjoyed on black bread.

People did not drink much milk on its own but used it in coffee or as a base for vegetable soups. Housewives also used milk for fresh curds that were used in sweet and savory pastas, dumplings, puddings, cheesecakes, and pancakes. Aged cheese was rarely used. In general, although dairy products were scarce they were a necessary part of the Eastern European diet in order to supplement the huge quantities of potatoes and provide necessary vitamins.

After the Middle Ages the Sephardi Jews lived mainly in a variety of Middle Eastern communities in which they used their history and current situation to enjoy a unique cuisine. Rice, flour, lentils, beans, olives, and cheeses were all household staples. Housewives made preserves from the peels of quinces, apricots, and lemons, and pieces of dry bread were soaked in water and oil and then combined with pepper and cheese and fried.

During the week in Jerusalem, Sephardi ate mainly soup (made of chickpeas, white beans, or some vegetables), beans, peas, lentils, noodles, and pastries. Beans were always eaten with rice and during the summer lettuce salads were popular, as were small side salads such as tomatoes mixed with cucumber, parsley, and hot pepper. People pickled eggplant and small lemons in oil, vinegar, and hot spices, and pasta dishes were popular in the summer. Snacks such as noodles with cheese, *burekas* filled with salted cheese, or spinach with hard-boiled eggs were common, as were soft cheeses. Fresh fish was rare and expensive in many places, but salt cod was soaked in water, then tomato juice, and served. Chicken was a luxury that was rarely consumed, but beef was regularly eaten as meat soup, or things like stuffed intestine or brains served with lemon, chopped meat, and marrow bones.

EARLY JEWISH AMERICAN HISTORY

The first Jews came to America in 1654 via Portugal and Recife, Brazil. However, it took many decades before a viable Jewish community began to take shape. In New York (then New Amsterdam) and in other coastal cities such as Newport, Rhode Island and Savannah, Georgia, synagogues were gradually established to meet communal needs. There is much research that shows evidence of small but thriving Jewish communities in the Northeast in the colonial, Revolutionary, and early national periods. America was particularly appealing for Jews immediately before and after the Revolutionary war because of the ideals of religious tolerance and freedom that were taking shape. However, Jews never formed more than one-tenth of one percent of the population during any of these periods. Newport, Philadelphia, Charleston, Savannah, and New York were among the first Jewish communities in the United States.

With newfound religious freedom the Jews had to struggle more than ever to balance their religious lives with their secular lives. The early 1800s marked the beginning of denominationalism in American Jewry. American Jews were beginning to take cues from Germany and other Jewish Enlightenment communities in Europe; they saw that Jewish philosophy and observance did not need only to be one predetermined way. People began to take new perspectives on how and why to observe the laws in order to better integrate into American society. Both the Reform and the Conservative movements started in Germany but moved with immigrants to America in this time. The new forms of Judaism were much more liberal than traditional Judaism, but their followers found a way to value Judaism while simultaneously valuing secular life.

The first large wave of Jewish immigrants came from Germany beginning in the 1830s to 1840s. Many German Jews were poverty-stricken and work conditions were difficult. Throughout Germany they faced discriminatory economic legislation that restricted them from certain trades and professions. Seeking to improve their lot, thousands of young Jews embarked for America. Although the German émigrés started off poor, they quickly built Jewish communities for themselves, worked in business, and joined the upper class. Many German Jews were involved in banking, commerce, and philanthropy, and they soon built clubs, synagogues, and other institutions.

Beginning in the 1860s there was a second wave of Jewish immigration from Eastern Europe to America that lasted into the beginning of the twentieth century. Jews from Poland, Russia, Lithuania, and many other countries came to the United States to escape the pogroms. Entire communities were being destroyed, and instead of trying to rebuild their homes, Eastern European Jews took a chance and boarded boats to America in large numbers.

Many Eastern European Jews settled in New York City, because that was the destination for most boats. However, there were many others who ventured to other established communities, both near and far. Eastern European Jews came to America with nothing and lived in squalor. The German Jews who had already established themselves formed help organizations for the immigrants, and family members and former village members helped new immigrants get settled. Again, although this group of immigrants started out poor, they slowly climbed the ranks of American society and achieved the American dream of middle class.

The food of this time was extremely similar to the food that the Jews ate in Eastern Europe. One could walk in a Jewish immigrant neighborhood and find herrings, pickles, smoked and spiced meats, produce, and bread and bagels sold from pushcarts or trays on the street. Eventually, predominantly Jewish neighborhoods like New York's Lower East Side and parts of south Philadelphia became more settled, and Jewish shops and eventually restaurants were established.

Jewish immigration into the United States continues to the present day. In the years leading up to and immediately following World War II, thousands of Jews took refuge in the United States; thousands more came in the 1980s and 1990s with the fall of East Germany and the Soviet Union, free to practice their religion in their new home. For centuries, when Jews abroad have needed to leave their adopted home they have found a place in the United States. Consequently, just as the United States, a country of immigrants, represents a microcosm of the world, so too does it represent a microcosm of world Jewry. Like Israel, the United States has representative citizens from throughout the Jewish world: Iran and the Middle East; Ethiopia, Egypt and Morocco; Eastern and Western Europe.

2

Major Foods and Ingredients

The foods and ingredients that Jewish Americans consume depend heavily on the region of descent of the individual and the current region in America in which one lives. To say that there is only one type of Jewish food or ingredient that belongs to one particular ethnicity would be to say that there is only one type of Jewish American who lives in one region in America and whose ancestors are from only one place.

Jewish Americans are as diverse as all Americans in current and past living situations. Jewish Americans may be from families who immigrated from Russia, Poland, Hungary, Israel, Iran, Iraq, Syria, Lebanon, Germany, Ethiopia, Italy, Holland, France, Spain, or elsewhere. Those families may have come to the United States many generations ago or even just a few days ago. They may be observant or secular. They may keep kosher or not. They may feel and identify as strongly culturally Jewish or they may identify as primarily American or as a so-called hyphenated American from their country of ancestry or origin, as Ethiopian-American first, for example, and Jewish-American second.

Further, the United States itself is a vast and diverse nation. Americans on the East Coast do not necessarily have the same diets as those in the Midwest, the South, the Southwest, the West Coast or the Pacific Northwest. While some foods are available nationally, others are regional or local in origin and availability.

There are some things that bind all types of Jewish American food. First, there is some attention paid to the laws of kashrut or other typical Jewish eating customs, even if they are not prepared in complete agreement with the traditional laws of kashrut. So while a nonkosher Jew may eat pork or a cheeseburger, pork or a cheeseburger would not be likely candidates to be considered a Jewish food. Second, many of the typical Jewish foods and ingredients have strong associations with Jewish holidays, such as potato latkes or jelly doughnuts for Hanukkah. These foods may be eaten year round in both secular and religious contexts but their Jewishness may come from their important role on the Jewish holiday table. Their preparation may vary regionally. Finally, despite regional and ancestral differences among Jewish Americans there is always a style of cooking representative of the older generation and a style of cooking representative of the newer generation.

There are many dishes and ingredients that qualify as Jewish foods. Though this is largely dependent on region, the age of the cook, and more, one can look at the following as a relatively representative explanation of major Jewish American foods and ingredients.

GRAINS AND STARCHES

Barley

Barley is a grain available in many forms with a variety of applications. The most common barley that Jewish Americans cook with is pearled barley, which is hulled, polished barley. Barley is used in many different dishes in Jewish American cooking, primarily in Ashkenazi kitchens. Barley may be thrown in with *cholent*, a Shabbat meat and bean stew, or may be cooked stovetop like rice and made into a flavorful pilaf, sometimes called "toasted barley." Also, cooks commonly use barley in a warming mushroom barley soup.

Kasha

Jewish Americans, especially those of Russian ancestry, eat kasha, which is the grain of the buckwheat plant. The grains are called buckwheat groats. Whether the groats are sold whole or cut into fine or coarse pieces determines the texture and cooking time. Many Jewish Americans use the Russian language name *kasha* not only to refer to buckwheat groats, but also to other cooked grains such as millet or oats. Kasha and bowties, also referred to as kasha *varnishkes*, is a side dish or entree made with egg noodles or plain noodles, usually bowties. The noodles and kasha are traditionally combined with onion, garlic, chicken fat, and egg. Sometimes mushrooms are added. This dish is a typical accompaniment to meat meals. Another popular kasha preparation is kasha pilaf, in which the kasha grains are toasted and coated with egg and then cooked along with mushroom and onion with water or broth for a finished dish that resembles rice pilaf. Buckwheat has a strong and distinctive flavor.

Potatoes

Potatoes are commonly used in Jewish American cooking—especially Ashkenazi cooking with Eastern European influences—as the main starch for a meal. Potatoes are frequently added to soups or stews and are often served simply roasted with oil, salt, and pepper as a side dish. Another popular preparation for potatoes is potato kugel. Kugel is a catch-all term used to denote a starch-based dish baked in a casserole then cut into squares and served. Potato kugel is made with grated potatoes, onion, egg, and seasoning and baked into a sort of casserole cake with an abundance of oil. It is a popular side dish with meats. A similar preparation of grated potato, when fried in pancakes, makes the latke, an important Hanukkah food. Whether in a kugel, latke, or on their own, potatoes are so frequently used because they go well as a side with a variety of meals that Jewish Americans eat. Another common Jewish American food made with potatoes, eaten as an appetizer, snack or lunch, is the potato knish. Potato knishes are mashed seasoned potatoes (traditionally flavored with schmaltz, chicken fat) that are wrapped with dough and then fried or baked. In New York City and elsewhere in the United States they are sold on the street, popular with Jews and non-Jews alike.

Potato Kugel

6 potatoes, grated	1 tsp salt
1 large onion, grated	1/2 tsp pepper
2 TBSP flour or	1/4 c. vegetable oil or
matzah meal	schmaltz, divided
2 eggs	Paprika to taste

Preheat oven to 400 degrees. Grate potatoes and drain. Mix in onion, flour, eggs, and seasoning. Put about half the oil in a casserole dish and heat in oven, about 10 minutes. Pour mixture into casserole. Sprinkle remaining oil and paprika on top. Bake about one hour, until brown and cooked through.

Rice

Rice is the most common starch for Jewish Americans of Sephardi descent and is used in a multitude of ways. Sephardi Jews often use rice as the base for a stuffing to stuff either meat or vegetables. Often, rice is commonly simply cooked as a pilaf and serves as a hearty side dish or cooked in pilaf style with the addition of many ingredients such as tomatoes, almonds, peas, or olives. Rice may also be used in desserts such as rice puddings or even cakes.

Rye

Jewish rye bread is the bread of choice for Jewish Americans when eating traditional deli sandwiches and other preparations. It is made from a mixture of rye flour and wheat and can vary in color depending on the ingredients. Traditional Jewish rye bread is actually a sourdough bread made with a relatively small amount of rye flour and speckled with caraway seeds.

Teff

Injera is a staple bread of Ethiopian and Eritrean Jews. *Injera* is a large pancake-type bread made from a soured (fermented) batter of flour made from the grain teff. In many cases wheat flour is added to the batter as well. Pieces of *injera* are used to pick up pieces of cooked meat or vegetables and whole *injera* are used to line platters and are eaten, soaked in sauces from the foods placed on top, at the end of the meal.

Wheat

Although wheat and wheat products are not a common side dish in Jewish American cuisine, wheat flour is used to make many different baked goods, including challah, the Shabbat bread, matzah, noodles, and bagels. One of the signature dishes using wheat as a grain (rather than as wheat flour) is tabbouleh, a Middle Eastern salad popular in Israel and throughout the Arab world that combines abundant amounts of parsley, tomato, and cucumber with cooked bulgur wheat. Tabbouleh is typically eaten as an accompaniment to falafel, fried balls of chickpeas and spices, or meats like grilled lamb.

WHEAT PRODUCTS

Bagels

Bagels are a doughnut-shaped yeast roll with a dense, chewy texture and shiny crust. They are boiled in water before they are baked. Although plain bagels are popular, many bagel bakeries make plain, poppy seed, sesame seed, garlic, onion, cinnamon raisin, egg, salt, everything bagels, and so on. The traditional way to enjoy a bagel is with lox (smoked salmon) and cream cheese. Bagels are eaten by many Americans and are no longer perceived as a particularly Jewish food but are still an important element on the Ashkenazi Jewish table.

Challah

Challah is a brioche-like egg bread that American Jews from all regions eat on Shabbat. It is made with either white or whole wheat flour (depending on one's focus on nutrition) and honey or sugar. Many Jewish Americans use the leftovers from the Shabbat challah to make French toast with thick slices of challah bread on Sunday mornings.

Couscous

Couscous is often misidentified as a grain in and of itself. Actually it is a type of miniature pasta made from semolina wheat flour and water just like other dried pasta shapes. It is traditionally eaten by Jewish Americans who are of Moroccan, Israeli, Iraqi, or other Middle Eastern heritage, but is popular among Jewish Americans of other backgrounds as well. Couscous is traditionally steamed over a lamb or vegetable stew but can also be prepared pilaf style like rice. Depending on one's preference one may use Moroccan couscous, which is granular semolina pasta, or Israeli couscous, which are slightly larger, round pasta balls. Couscous is often cooked plain or with spices added and is then used as a base for meat dishes or stews to seep up the sauce.

Egg Noodles and Pasta

Egg noodles are dried pasta that is made with either eggs or egg whites and are most commonly used in Jewish American cooking in kugels as well as in soups and as a side dish. Different shapes and sizes of egg noodles are customarily used for different kinds of kugels. For example, thin spaghetti-like egg noodles are used in Jerusalem kugel (sweet and peppery), while wider spiral noodles are often used for apple kugel and flat noodles are used for cheese kugel.

Dried pasta made without eggs is used in a few Jewish dishes like kasha and bowties and is also a popular addition to soups.

Mildred's Dairy Noodle Kugel

Noodles

1 lb. fine egg noodles, cooked	1 lb. cottage cheese
1 1/2 pints sour cream, 1 cup reserve	2 oz. butter
	1 1/2 c. sugar
3 large or 4 medium eggs, beaten	1 TBSP salt

(continued)

Topping

1/2 c. dark brown sugar
2 tsp cinnamon
2 c. chopped walnuts
2 TBSP very soft butter

Preheat oven to 325 degrees. Mix noodles, 1 pint sour cream, sugar, salt, eggs, and cottage cheese in bowl until just combined. Pour into buttered 9 × 13 pan and top with pats of butter and reserved 1/2 pint of sour cream in dollops. Bake, covered with foil, 90 minutes.

Make topping. Combine brown sugar, walnuts, cinnamon, and soft butter and mix with hands, ensuring that the walnuts are covered in the remaining ingredients. Remove foil and top kugel with mixture. Bake another 1/2 hour.

Matzah

Matzah (often spelled matzoh or matzo) is an unleavened cracker that is meant to be eaten on the holiday of Passover. It may be made by hand or by machine and its quick preparation in under 18 minutes (the number 18 symbolizes life in the Jewish tradition) ensures that yeast has not begun the fermentation and leavening process. The tradition of eating matzah hearkens back to the Jews' exodus from Egypt. They left for their journey with unleavened bread as they could not take time to allow bread to rise. During the Passover holiday, Jews are obligated to eat matzah instead of bread and other grain products and often make preparations like desserts from matzah flour called matzah meal.

Many Jews eat matzah year round and there are many matzah products that Jewish Americans frequently use in daily and holiday cooking. One of the most quintessential Jewish American foods is matzah balls, which are made with matzah meal or matzah ball mix, eggs, and oil and cooked like a dumpling in boiling water or broth. Then after they are cooked the matzah balls are eaten with traditional chicken soup. Another matzah preparation is matzah farfel, crumbles of matzah cooked in a kugel or as a Passover stuffing. Finally, matzah *brei* or fried matzah is a preparation popular for Passover breakfasts or dairy dinners in which matzah pieces are coated with egg and fried similar to French toast. Matzah *brei* is often eaten with jelly and/or sour cream. Also honey, salt and pepper, cream cheese, applesauce, or garlic powder are popular accompaniments. A savory matzah *brei* has the addition of onions and possibly schmaltz, whereas a sweet version uses cinnamon and sugar.

Passover Matzah Stuffing

2 sticks margarine	1 box matzah, finely broken
2 eggs	1/4 tsp pepper
1 medium onion, minced	1 c. kosher wine
1 tsp salt	1 1/2 c. chicken broth

In a large frying pan, sauté onion in margarine until translucent. Add matzah and toast lightly. Remove from heat. In a separate bowl combine remaining ingredients. Add to pan. Stuffing can be used to stuff poultry or can be baked separately in a 350 degree oven, about 40 minutes.

LEGUMES

Chickpeas

Although chickpeas, also known as *nahit*, originated as a Middle Eastern food, they are now common in all types of Jewish American cooking. The chickpea is a firm and nutty-tasting legume that is high in protein. Middle Eastern American Jews often use either canned or dried chickpeas to make hummus, which is pureed chickpeas combined with sesame paste and other ingredients. Another common use of chickpeas is falafel, which are fried balls of seasoned chickpea dough. Eastern European American Jews of course will also eat and make these dishes; however, they more traditionally use chickpeas in *cholent*, a vegetarian or meat stew eaten on Shabbat.

Hummus

1 16 oz. can of chickpeas or garbanzo beans	2 TBSP olive oil
	juice of one-half lemon
2 cloves garlic	salt to taste
1/4 c. liquid from can of chickpeas	2 TBSP tahini

Combine ingredients in blender or food processor until smooth. If desired olive oil can be omitted from the mix and poured on top as garnish.

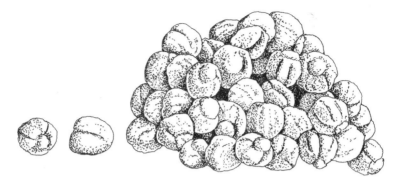

Chickpeas. © J. Susan Cole Stone.

Lentils

The lentil is of importance to Sephardi Jews, especially those of the Middle East. It is often used in soups and stews.

FRUITS

Canned Fruit

Jewish Americans use canned fruits in a multitude of ways. Some people use cherry pie filling to stuff hamantaschen, a Purim pastry, while others use it to add something more to a packaged cake mix. Also, many Jewish Americans add maraschino cherries or canned pineapple to their kugels, or use different fruits in syrup as a topping for blintzes.

Dried Fruit

Dried peaches, apples, apricots, dates, prunes, pears, and raisins among other things are a common feature of the Jewish American pantry, especially but by no means exclusively among Sephardi Jews. It is common for the host of a holiday meal, Shabbat dinner, or general dinner party to put out dishes of dried apricots or apples alongside nuts or chocolate as a snack before or after dinner. Jewish American cooks also often add prunes, apricots, or raisins to briskets and other braised meat dishes. Finally, there is a traditional Eastern European dessert called compote, which is a stewed mixture of fresh and dried fruits sometimes eaten as a warm fruit stew and sometimes drunk as a cold sweet beverage.

VEGETABLES

Beets

Jewish Americans who have ancestors from Russia or Poland commonly use beets when making many different types of borscht. Although it is becoming increasingly easy to find a multitude of colors and sizes in beets, borscht is generally made with large red beets. It may be served cold or hot and may be made with meat (generally flanken, beef short ribs) or dairy ingredients, such as sour cream.

Carrots

Carrots are used in two primary ways in Jewish American cooking. One way they are used is similar to how onions are used; they provide background flavor to soups and sauces. Almost all Jewish chicken soup recipes, Eastern and Western European, include carrots. However, carrots are also featured as the main ingredient in many dishes. Tzimmes, a common dish for Rosh Hashana and Shabbat, is carrots cooked with honey or another sweetening agent and a variety of other ingredients such as raisins. Moroccan Jewish Americans boil carrots and spice them to be eaten as an appetizer salad.

Eggplant

Eggplant is primarily a Sephardi ingredient, specifically used by Jewish Americans of Middle Eastern descent. One of the most common applications for eggplant is *baba ganoush*, a roasted and pureed eggplant spread that is flavored with tahini (sesame paste), garlic, and lemon. Sephardi American Jews also often stuff eggplants or sauté eggplant pieces for a simple side dish.

Green Beans and Broccoli

Green vegetables were not common in traditional food circles in either Sephardi or Ashkenazi cooking. Old-school Jewish American cooks are known to overcook their green vegetables into oblivion, and they are usually dwarfed on one's plate by huge quantities of meat and grains. However, one common green vegetable dish on Jewish American tables is a green bean or broccoli casserole. Mushroom soup is combined with frozen green beans or broccoli, alongside fried onions and other seasonings, and then baked. It should be noted, however, that modern Jewish American cooks make the same health-conscious vegetable dishes that many other Americans make, such as steamed asparagus or sautéed spinach.

Onions

As in many other cuisines, onions are at the center of countless Ashkenazi and Sephardi dishes. The onion is not used as a primary ingredient in Jewish cooking. Rather, it is used to provide a rich background flavor and to intensify soups, sauces, meats, and starch dishes.

Pickled Vegetables

Pickled vegetables were once mainly a food of necessity—a way to preserve fresh vegetables through the winter in times before supermarket frozen food and ample refrigeration. Nevertheless, pickles made from a variety of vegetables have become important parts of the American Jewish diet, valued for their flavors as much as their preservation properties. It is tough to imagine a delicatessen beef hot dog without a topping of sauerkraut, which is pickled cabbage. Likewise, it is tough to imagine a corned beef sandwich without a small side of coleslaw, a much lighter pickle of cabbage salad. Dill and half sour (brined but not cooked) pickles made from cucumbers, tomatoes, and beets are important foods of the Ashkenazi table, often served as sides with every main meal. Sephardi pickles include olives, chiles, carrots, and peppers.

MEATS

Because many animals, like pork and hunted game and many cuts of meat, are not kosher, this section focuses on widely consumed kosher meats. However, American Jews, depending on their level of religious observance, may eat many other meats as well.

Beef

Beef is surely the most common of the meats for Jewish Americans. Beef brisket, braised in the style of a pot roast, is a centerpiece of many holiday meals. Flanken or short ribs is another popular braised item. Beef shank, like veal, is the basis of many soups or stews. Grilled or broiled beefsteak and hamburgers are popular among Jewish Americans as they are for many other meat-eating Americans.

A number of other preparations are made from pickling or smoking beef. Since pork is not kosher, many lunchmeat products usually made from pork such as bologna, salami, or liverwurst have kosher equivalents made from beef, or less often, chicken or turkey. Popular Jewish delicatessen items made from beef, like hot dogs, corned beef (pickled beef brisket), pastrami (pickled peppered beef brisket), and, to a lesser extent, tongue (pickled beef tongue) are popular delicatessen items for both Jewish and non-Jewish Americans.

Many beef items in Jewish cuisine developed as acceptable alternatives to nonkosher foods. For example, a popular Eastern European dish is blood sausage, nonkosher for its use of blood, most often from the pig. An alternative not popular outside the Jewish community is kishka, a beef intestine stuffed with a filling of matzah meal and fat (schmaltz). Similarly, and perhaps more palatably to some, Polish stuffed cabbage, usually stuffed with chopped pork and rice, has its Jewish equivalent stuffed with beef.

Lamb

Although lamb is not one of the most common meats that Jewish Americans use, it does have a place on holiday and Shabbat tables, especially among Sephardi Jews with cultural connections to the Mediterranean, North Africa, and the Middle East. One of the symbolic foods of the holiday of Passover is lamb, particularly lamb shanks, and so this is a common dish to make for this holiday. Sephardi Jews often also make stuffed lamb shoulder or grilled lamb kebabs.

Veal

The meat of a calf, veal has many kosher cuts and is popular sautéed or braised. Veal flanken or short ribs are delicious on the grill or braised, and the shank is the base of many soups and stews.

Other Meats

There are other kosher meats less widely consumed. Deer, when farm raised, can produce kosher venison. Venison is not a large part of the Jewish American diet, or, for that matter the Jewish diet anywhere, but has begun to make inroads on kosher fine dining menus. Another potentially kosher meat is goat, which is valued more for its milk to make cheese than for its meat among Jewish Americans. Nevertheless, goat serves as an interesting alternative for Jewish Americans and is consumed by Jewish Americans with cultural ties to North Africa and parts of the Middle East.

POULTRY

Chicken

American Jews consume a large variety of poultry, at the center of which is the chicken. Chicken is main protein of the typical Shabbat meal, often in the form of "chicken in the pot," a two-course meal in which a whole chicken is simmered. First, chicken soup with matzah balls or noodles is eaten and following that, pieces of boiled chicken with carrots and potatoes form a main course. Roast chicken is also a popular meal. The liver of the chicken is important in the Jewish appetizer chopped liver, in which sautéed chicken livers, onions, and schmaltz (chicken fat) are pureed and served on crackers. Chicken is king for many meals, including breaded cutlets, sautéed, stewed, and grilled chicken preparations.

Turkey, Duck, and Cornish Hen

Other kosher birds pale to the chicken in terms of quantity of consumption but are important and often tied to particular holidays. Like most Americans, Jewish Americans consume turkey at Thanksgiving. Kosher turkey is widely available and a roast turkey breast may be a substitute for Shabbat chicken and sliced turkey a popular lunch meat. Roast duck is traditionally served on Rosh Hashanah, the Jewish New Year. Its fatty succulence and preparation with sweet flavors represent an auspicious start for a rich and sweet New Year. Finally, Cornish hen is popular for catered events like weddings and bar mitzvahs due to its ready portioning for individual plates.

FISH

Carp

The mild, fleshy carp is found on the table at nearly every Jewish holiday or event in the form of gefilte fish, large poached quenelles of ground carp, eggs, matzah meal, and seasonings. Gefilte fish is often accompanied by carrots and is eaten with chopped horseradish. While many varieties of prepared canned and frozen gefilte fish are available, countless American Jews have been traumatized by the sight of their mothers and grandmothers killing a carp in the bathtub and grinding it in the kitchen.

Herring

Herring is of extreme importance for Ashkenazi Jews. Once an inexpensive and reliable source of high-quality protein for poor Jews of Eastern Europe, for American Ashkenazi Jews, the fish has achieved iconic status. Often prepared pickled with salt, vinegar, or both and served with onions along with a sauce made from milt for a meat meal or sour cream for a dairy meal, herring is a salty oily taste of the past. Appetizing stores (Jewish stores specializing in smoked and preserved fish) like Russ and Daughters on New York City's Lower East Side still prepare and sell herring in the traditional way.

Gefilte Fish

1 lb. ground whitefish	1 tsp salt
1 c. water	1/4 c. sugar
1 lb. ground pike	1/2 onion, grated
1/2 tsp pepper	2 TBSP matzah meal
4 eggs	2 qt. fish or vegetable stock

Mix all ingredients. Shape into loaves and poach in stock about 90 minutes. Let cool in stock. Then remove from stock and slice into portions.

Salmon

Fresh salmon fillet is a healthy and popular entrée for American Jews. But salted salmon in the form of lox (from the Scandinavian gravlax), kippered salmon, and smoked salmon have special importance for American Jews. Often paired with bagels, cream cheese, raw onion, tomato, and olives for a Shabbat dairy lunch, leisurely Sunday breakfast, or quick weekday dinner, the bagel and lox is an icon of Jewish food.

Whitefish and Sable

Along with smoked salmon, lox, and herring, smoked whitefish and sable are prominent on fish platters, eaten with bagels in the same way as lox.

SEASONINGS

Seasoning practices among American Jews are as diverse as American Jewry itself. Again, depending on cultural and family traditions, seasonings from around the world of the Jewish Diaspora may be invoked. Consider for example the Shabbat dinner of chicken. Different American Jewish families may prepare the following meals:

• Eastern European (generally Ashkenazi) roast chicken flavored with salt, pepper, paprika and onion soup mix served with roast potatoes.
• Mediterranean (generally Sephardi) sautéed chicken pieces seasoned with garlic, olive oil, and lemon with rice pilaf topped with toasted almonds.
• Ethiopian *doro wat*, chicken and hard-boiled eggs cooked in *berbere* chili paste and onions. Served with *injera*.

- Persian *fesenjan*, chicken cooked with walnuts and pomegranate seeds. Served with rice.
- Israeli chicken fried with *zatar*, an herb and sesame mixture, served with pita and chickpea salad.

Just as there is no typical American Jew there is no typical American Jewish seasoning.

However, there are a few seasonings especially predominant in Ashkenazi American cooking that deserve special mention.

Onion Soup Mix

Powdered onion soup mix, either in bouillon or loose form, is a popular and quick Jewish American method for seasoning meats, vegetables, and starches. Cooks frequently use onion soup mix powder dry or in combination with oil to produce an extremely flavorful and salty dish. Mushroom soup mix may be used in the same way.

Pepper

Traditional Jewish American cooking is often relatively bland, or, to be charitable, mild. However, pepper is one seasoning that Jewish American cooks are not afraid to use a lot of. Gefilte fish, kugels, vegetable dishes, and potatoes are often seasoned heavily with ground black pepper.

Schmaltz

Schmaltz, rendered chicken fat, often cooked with onions, is a quintessential Ashkenazi seasoning. It has fallen out of fashion somewhat with increasing concern about consumption of saturated fats and the advent of cheap pareve (kosher for both meat and dairy meals) fats like vegetable shortening. Because schmaltz is made from meat, it is an important substitute for butter in traditional meat meals such as roast chicken with mashed potatoes.

DAIRY

Cottage Cheese

Although many Jewish Americans have lactose intolerance, dairy ingredients like cottage cheese are extremely popular. Cottage cheese or a similar but firmer cheese, farmer's cheese, is used in kugels, blintzes, cottage cheese pancakes, and a variety of desserts.

Cream Cheese

Cream cheese is either eaten simply smeared (or in Yiddish, as a *schmear*) on a bagel with other toppings or is used in baking cheese cakes, *rugelach*, kugels, and other sweet treats.

Sour Cream

Sour cream has many applications in the Jewish American kitchen. It may be added to cold borscht to make it creamy, or to hot blintzes with cherry sauce. It too is used in kugels and also in many different Jewish desserts, especially Jewish apple cake.

FATS

Margarine

Margarine is probably the most popular fat used by Jewish Americans. There are many brands of nondairy margarine that make it easy for Jews to make dishes that conventionally include butter. Although margarine surely does not have as rich of a taste as butter (and although it may be composed of trans fats) margarine is a perfect substitute for any dessert dishes that call for butter, as well as any number of other recipes. Consequently, many Jewish American cooks rarely use butter and do not keep it in their homes.

Olive Oil

Sephardi Jewish Americans use olive oil as their primary fat when cooking, and sometimes even baking. Virgin and extra virgin olive oil are commonly used to sauté vegetables, roast meat, and make some types of cookies.

Schmaltz

Schmaltz, sufficiently important to be mentioned as a seasoning as well as a fat, is rendered chicken or goose fat that is used for frying, spreading on bread, or simply as an addition to meat recipes. Today schmaltz is sold in Jewish grocery stores in a jar and is ready to use. However, there are still some Jewish Americans who make their own schmaltz by taking chicken or goose fat and melting it in a pan, usually with onions. After most of the fat has been extracted the melted fat is strained and separated from the crispy pieces, known to southern Americans as cracklins and to Jewish Americans as a snack called *gribenes*.

Shortening

Shortening, often referred to by its brand name, is a common fat for Jewish Americans to use because it resembles lard and other greases but is vegetarian. There are very few savory Jewish American dishes that make use of the fat, opting for schmaltz or margarine instead; however, pastries and other fat-based desserts often include vegetable shortening.

DESSERTS

Desserts in American Jewish cooking are complicated by the prohibition against eating meat and dairy together in kosher law. Since many festive and holiday meals are meat-centered, the dessert that caps off the evening needs to be pareve, meaning it cannot contain dairy like milk, cheese, or butter, or animal products rendering it acceptable for both meat and dairy meals.

Because butter is a common ingredient in many desserts, pareve desserts use vegetable shortening or margarine as a substitute. With concern about the consumption of artificial trans fats, still another substitute is desirable. Transfat-free shortenings are now widely available in the market.

A visit to a kosher bakery is a multisensory experience that will not be quickly forgotten. Rich chocolate, cinnamon, and glazed items abound. Some key Jewish desserts are:

Rugelach: a cream cheese pastry rolled around a filling of chocolate, jam, or nuts.
Babka: a cake loaded with chocolate or cinnamon and sugar.
Jewish apple cake: often a sour cream-based cake with cinnamon and apples.
Jelly doughnuts: an important Hanukkah desert in the Sephardi community.
Honey cake: a cake soaked in honey for a sweet New Year.
Dried fruit and nuts: a traditional accompaniment to the main dessert at the end of a
  meal.

Rosh Hashanah Honey Cake

Honey cake is a typical finish to the Rosh Hashanah meal, eaten with hopes for a sweet New Year.

8 eggs, separated	2 tsp baking powder
1 tsp vanilla	1 c. honey
2 c. sugar	1 tsp baking soda
4 c. flour	1 c. coffee
1 c. vegetable oil	1 c. chopped nuts, optional

Preheat oven to 375 degrees. In a large bowl mix sugar and oil. Add egg yolks one at a time. Add honey, nuts, coffee, and vanilla. When mixed sift in dry ingredients. In a separate bowl or mixer, beat egg whites until stiff. Fold into batter. Pour into greased 9 × 13 pan or two loaf pans. Bake about one hour.

BEVERAGES

In general Jewish Americans drink the same sort of beverages as any other American. There are a few points of interest. First, most beverages are kosher in and of themselves, but it is important to remember that the prohibition against combining meat and dairy also applies to beverages. So a kosher meat meal that ends with coffee and tea will be accompanied by nondairy creamer.

American Jews do consume alcohol, especially beer, wine (kosher wine is available), and whiskey. Toasting, by proclaiming *l'chaim,* "to life," with scotch or schnapps is an important holiday ritual for festive holidays including Shabbat (usually at the kiddush after services), and important life cycle events like *bris* (circumcision), bar mitzvah, and weddings.

One beverage deserves special mention: the egg cream, an iconic American Jewish beverage that contains neither egg nor cream. Purportedly invented on New York City's Lower East Side in the early 1900s, the egg cream consists of U-Bet brand chocolate syrup, milk, and seltzer and is a cheap alternative to a milkshake or malted milk popular at the time. A good egg cream can still be found in New York City, and while other flavors like vanilla and strawberry are available, purists insist on chocolate.

3

Cooking

The act of cooking in a Jewish home may be a communal one and sometimes even a sacred one. Although weekday cooking is important to any Jewish home, what matters most for the Jewish American cook (and the Jewish American eater) is holiday and Shabbat (Sabbath) cooking, where the time and preparation required is an important part of the ritual of readying for the holy days. Jews share a special relationship with food, and this relationship is expressed not only in all aspects of the food itself, but also in all aspects of food preparation and execution.

A discussion of cooking takes into account the diversity of American Jews and therefore of American Jewish cooking. There are American Jews who are not observant and do not cook Jewish food. There are those who do not practice the religion but who cook traditional Jewish foods for holidays. There are those who are religious and observe the laws of kashrut but who do not necessarily cook, and there are those who are both observant and cook. Further, Jewish cooking has a wide repertoire across the many cultures that Jews temporarily called home in the Diaspora: Eastern Europe, Poland, Spain, Italy, Persia (now Iran), Syria, Lebanon, Egypt, Ethiopia, and, of course, the United States, among others. The predominance of the Ashkenazi flavors of Eastern Europe in our vision of American Jewish food traditions—blintzes, kugel, brisket, tzimmes, matzah ball soup, bagels and lox—is largely attributable to the predominance of the immigration of these Jews over that of the Jews of the many other cultures mentioned.

WHO COOKS?

Traditional Judaism is a patriarchal society and separates the roles of men and women very clearly. In the most observant and traditional of circles the men study Torah and the commentaries (Talmud and others) every day and the women perform household duties, including keeping the household clean and organized, raising the children, and doing anything having to do with food. There are still a number of American Jews who practice this division of labor, particularly in the most observant communities. Other American Jews, of course, have two-income households, men as primary caregivers, or other arrangements found in American society in general.

Although the patriarchal arrangement is no longer the exact case in most Jewish American homes, there are many traditional families who view the woman as the primary cook, regardless of her other obligations or employment status. Even many households who spurn tradition in other ways—both mother and father working, driving or working on the Sabbath, or not attending synagogue, for example—may expect the matriarch of the family to be responsible for meal planning and preparation, especially at times of holidays or special occasions. Traditionally the woman of the house is the one who cooks meals, particularly those for Shabbat and holidays.

There may be some further explanation as to why the woman is traditionally in charge of cooking in the Jewish home. First, it is relevant to note that in Jewish tradition, making challah, special Shabbat bread, is one of women's three responsibilities as a Jew. Challah itself is generally a round or braided bread enriched with eggs prepared specifically for the Sabbath but eaten on the Sabbath and any other time. Challah is not only essential for a Shabbat meal, it can be interpreted to symbolize all food, just as manna did for the Jews wandering the dessert in the Bible. So in traditional circles it may be seen that because it is the woman's responsibility to prepare the challah, meaning food in general by interpretation, it is the Jewish woman's responsibility to prepare all foods. The Jewish woman is traditionally thought to be responsible for her household, and part of this responsibility includes feeding the members of the household good kosher food.

There are additional textual explanations for why women are traditionally the primary cooks in the home. The book of Proverbs includes a 22-verse poem known commonly as "Eshet Chayil" or "Woman of Valor." This is an ancient hymn that men traditionally sing to their wives at the Shabbat table. It is about how the woman is in charge of taking care of the household and "gives food to her household and a portion to her maidservants" (Proverbs 31:10–31).

Additionally, in the Mishnah, a third-century rabbinic text, it says, "These are the tasks that a wife must carry out for her husband: she must grind corn

Woman making challah. Courtesy of
Rabbi Moshe and Meira Saks.

and bake and do washing and cooking" (Mishnah, Nashim, Ketubot 5). This text has influenced the way in which the Jewish woman is perceived and has influenced Jews to understand the woman's role as not only the maker of the challah, but by extension the maker of all food.

Although all of this is traditionally true, American Jews are eschewing these traditions more and more each year. As Jewish women—even highly observant and traditional Jewish women—are beginning to enter the workplace, it is becoming more common for couples to share the duties of cooking in the house. While it is rare for a man to make challah in the traditional Jewish home, it is increasingly common for the man to make much or all of everyday meals and even be involved in some or all of the preparation of Shabbat and holiday dinners. It should also be said that the children in the household—especially girls and young women—are likely to participate in the cooking as well.

One cannot understand who cooks in a Jewish American kitchen without a mention of the stereotype—and reality—of the Jewish American grand-mother. In many families the grandmother remains the main cook in the family, especially for holiday and special occasion meals where it may be unthinkable for a new bride to make or host the holiday dinner for the extended family. Jewish American grandmothers command a great deal of respect in the kitchen generally because of their extensive knowledge of old-world cuisine. It is not uncommon for an entire family to go to the grandmother's (and grandfather's) house for a holiday meal. They can often be relied upon for a delicious taste of the past. While grandmothers may pass their recipes on to their children and grandchildren, many choose to modernize recipes or to simply not make them at all. However, in the Jewish American community there is a definite gravitas when one informs those at a dinner party that "this is my grandmother's recipe!"

JEWISH AMERICAN APPROACH TO COOKING

Although Jewish Americans cook much of the same food as other Americans, depending on their level of acculturation and observance, their approach to that food is often quite interesting. Because of the boundaries placed on chefs from the kashrut laws and because of other cultural norms, a Jewish American kitchen does not always look like other American kitchens.

The second freezer (and/or refrigerator) is a fixture in many Jewish American homes. (It is usually located in the basement or the garage where there is more storage space.) In most areas of the country large varieties of kosher meat are not available at the local grocery store. Those who keep kosher in the home must travel some distance to find kosher meat in a grocery store, make a special trip to the local (or not so local) butcher, or order large quantities of meat from the closest kosher butcher (who is in some cases hundred of miles away). For this reason, American Jews tend to buy meat in large quantities and freeze it. They then defrost chicken or a roast as they need it.

In addition to using additional freezers to store extra meat, Jewish Americans often cook meals in the hopes of having leftovers to freeze. There are a number of reasons for this. First, those who do not live near many kosher restaurants and do not eat out in nonkosher restaurants may get sick of cooking every day and want an easy meal to defrost quickly. Also, a large part of Jewish American culture is entertaining large groups of people for holidays or Shabbat. Although the host or hostess customarily makes a guest list in advance, it is not uncommon to have last-minute guests. With extra food in the freezer the Jewish American chef does not need to worry about these extra guests being an imposition.

Additional refrigerators are also a common feature in Jewish American homes. The reason that people have additional refrigerators is simply to store extra food. This is intertwined with another common feature of the Jewish America approach to cooking. At a Jewish American dinner table there is usually an over-abundance of food, both in quantity and variety.

Meat at Park East Kosher Butcher in New York City. Courtesy of Rachel Saks.

Some observant Jews have separate ovens, separate refrigerators and freezers, or even entirely separate kitchens to observe the letter of the law in the kashrut requirement to separate meat and dairy. While one can observe kashrut by, for example, storing meat and dairy in separate parts of the same refrigerator, the more spatial separation there can be, the easier it is to consistently observe this law.

COOKING EQUIPMENT AND UTENSILS

Jewish Americans use the same cooking equipment and utensils during the week as any other American home cook. However, because of the constraints that Shabbat and holidays place on food and cooking, there are a number of different types of equipment and utensils that are Jewish or are common for Jews to use.

Traditional Jews do not cook on Shabbat, from Friday at sundown until Saturday at sundown; however, that does not mean that they cannot have hot food. Cooks must find a way to cook the food before Shabbat and keep it warm. In fact, many traditional Jewish dishes, such as *cholent*, a thick beef, barley, and bean porridge, originated in this practice of letting things slowly cook with residual heat from the start of the Sabbath on. For Shabbat dinner people commonly make food right before the Sabbath and ensure that it stays warm until it is time to eat it. However, there are times when whoever is cooking wants to make dinner ahead of time, or when people want a hot meal for Saturday lunch or dinner. There are three ways that traditional American Jews warm food or keep food warm. Of course, a nonobservant American Jew may simply heat or cook food on the Sabbath as she or he would any other day.

Crock-Pots are handy for making a stew or soup before Shabbat and keeping it warm until it is time to eat it. Kosher markets sell crock-pot liners, and there are many kosher Crock-pot recipes in circulation. Since the Sabbath restriction restricts turning on heat or lighting a fire during the Sabbath, as long as the crock-pot is plugged in and turned on before the start of the Sabbath it is acceptable. Still, some observant Jews consider it unacceptable as it is not a traditional cooking technique, only popular for the last half-century or so.

Crock-pot. © J. Susan Cole Stone.

Another option is to leave the food in the oven. Some Jewish Americans choose to leave their oven on throughout all of Shabbat at a temperature low enough to warm but not cook any of the food. Again since the oven is lit (turned on) before Shabbat, this is an appropriate heating method for observant Jews. Some new ovens—especially those marketed in Israel or in Jewish communities in the United States and elsewhere—actually now have a Sabbath mode. This oven setting does a number of things. First, it overrides the protective setting on most ovens that makes the oven and stovetop turn off after 12 hours of consecutive use, since it could not be turned back on during Shabbat. Second, it allows for a temperature low enough to sufficiently warm food but cool enough that the food is not being cooked.

Finally, a piece of equipment that is particular to the Jewish American kitchen is what is referred to as a *blech*. A *blech* is any hotplate, warming drawer, or stovetop cover that is used to keep foods warm. The most simple *blech* is a rectangular, covered, shallow pan filled with water and placed on the stovetop. Food is then placed atop it and slowly warms.

PREPARATION OF FOODS

Jewish American foods use the same food preparation techniques as American food in general: baking, roasting, stewing, simmering, frying, sautéing, grilling, steaming, broiling, and so on. As previously mentioned, visiting a typical Jewish American home on any given evening one may see American Jews, kosher or nonkosher, eating pizza, pasta, Chinese stir-fry, hamburgers, or nearly any other food, simply adapted to the laws of kashrut if the family is observant.

Because many traditional Jewish dishes have origins in Sabbath and holiday cooking traditions, when cooking during the holy day is prohibited, many Jewish foods are cooked slowly over a long period of time in a way that would be appropriate for a Sabbath or holiday meal. *Cholent, tzimmes,* and brisket are all common examples from the Ashkenazi tradition. Perhaps unfairly, Jewish foods have a reputation of being heavy, overcooked, and mildly flavored or bland, consistent with this type of cooking. And to some extent this is true. It is simply impossible for an observant Jew to make a fresh-tasting hot meal during the day of Shabbat or another major holiday, because nothing will have been able to be cooked since the previous afternoon.

However, a typical weekday will potentially show a variety of fresh-tasting food, influenced from a variety of Jewish and other cultures, and cooked using a variety of cooking techniques.

Cele's Holiday Brisket

Preheat oven to 450 degrees. Take:

1 beef brisket, cap removed, about 3–5 pounds

Sprinkle generously with:

2 TBSP salt   **3 TBSP paprika**
2 TBSP onion powder   **2 TBSP garlic powder**
1 tsp ground black pepper

Roast in a roasting pan in hot oven about 30 minutes or until browned.
Reduce heat to 325. Remove pan. Generously smear on brisket:

1 c. ketchup   **A few sprinkles of brown**
1/4 c. instant gravy powder   **gravy color**
2 TBSP Worcestershire   **1 packet onion soup mix**
  sauce

Add water to pan just until brisket is covered. Cover pan and braise about
three hours until very tender. Turn occasionally if you are worried about it.
Remove from oven and serve after a rest period of about 30 minutes. Can
also be made in advance, chilled, sliced, and served the next day.

Toasted "Barley" Brisket Accompaniment

1 lb. package barley-shaped pasta, cooked and drained
1 package onion soup mix
1 stick margarine, melted
1 can sliced mushrooms

Preheat oven to 350 degrees. Mix all ingredients together and place in casserole or large soufflé dish. Bake 30 minutes uncovered.

PROFESSIONAL COOKING

While women are the primary cooks at home, like elsewhere in the
United States, professional cooks are often men. Because food is so

important to the Jewish community, particularly among kosher Jews, many American Jews are entrepreneurs and workers in the food business. While one need not be a Jew to work in a kosher kitchen, as discussed in Chapter 5, Eating Out, a Jewish chef needs to light the ovens and there needs to be rabbinical supervision.

4

Typical Meals

During the week there are no particular meals or types of meals that Jewish Americans eat. Like so many other things, the types of foods that Jewish Americans eat and the times that they eat them depend almost entirely on where they live within the country, their family traditions, and what their personal preferences are. There are no particular laws governing what foods should be eaten for breakfast, lunch, or dinner, or when to eat those meals.

EATING TRADITIONS

Like any American family, Jewish Americans make much of family meals. Because the Shabbat is a major holy day observed weekly, many families, even those from less observant households, make it a point to eat together on Shabbat. In some families, Friday evening is reserved for a family Shabbat dinner at home with Saturday devoted to visits from the extended family, often at the home of the grandparents. Sunday meals are also special times for many Jewish American families since the Sabbath has ended but the secular workweek has not yet begun. While many observant Jews work Sunday through Thursday or Friday morning, American Jews who work outside of the Jewish community often have a second weekend day on Sunday that may be devoted to family meals at restaurants or other gatherings.

A weekday meal for American Jews sees the typical chaos of most American families. Juggling work, school, sports, and other after-school activities, an American Jewish family may eat at a restaurant, cook a meal using some convenience foods like frozen entrees or sides, or cook a quick dinner from scratch—eating patterns similar to those of many Americans.

Like many Americans, observant American Jews begin the meal with a prayer called the *ha'motzi*: "*Baruch atah Adonai eloheinu melech ha'olam, ha'motzi lechem min ha'aretz.* Blessed art thou, Lord our God, King of the Universe, who brings forth bread from the earth." In this prayer, bread is meant to stand for food in general, though there are also prayers specific to fruit, wine, and other foods. One meal ritual unique to American Jews is that while bread in the *ha'motzi* may be a symbolic representation of food in general, many observant Jews, and all Jews saying this prayer on Shabbat, tear off a piece of bread on its own and eat it following the *ha'motzi*. In this way, even though a full meal will follow, the first bite of the meal is a piece of bread over which the diner has said a blessing.

BLESSINGS

Before any meal traditional Jews first complete a ceremonial hand washing. This act is not meant to actually cleanse one's hands, but is intended to commemorate God's commandment to wash one's hands before and after certain activities, including eating. No soap is used in this activity; rather people traditionally fill a cup with a handle at a sink and splash water on each of their hands twice. The blessing is, "Blessed are You, Lord our God, King of the

Handwashing cup, also known as a laver. Courtesy of Rachel Saks.

universe, Who sanctified us with His commandments, and has commanded us to wash our hands." Of course, hands may be unceremoniously washed with soap for cleanliness before this ritual.

Following the hand washing the *ha'motzi* blessing is recited. While it should be noted that it is not likely that Jews will make a large meal and not include bread, because the *ha'motzi* is symbolic of all food and people usually want to mark that meal with the *ha'motzi* blessing, there are separate blessings that are commonly said over foods for which *ha'motzi* is not necessary. If a small breakfast of coffee and a muffin is enjoyed, or if a quick snack of a chocolate bar or potato chips is eaten, there are other blessings to recite. Table 4.1 is a list of all of the blessings that may be said over various foods if bread is not present. If bread is present, saying the *ha'motzi* eliminates the need to say the rest of these blessings. As a matter of course, Jews who are not highly observant but who nevertheless pray before eating may say *ha'motzi* before any meal.

After all meals or snacks, grace after meals, *birkat hamazon,* is recited. There are two different types of graces that can be said, one after eating a meal containing bread, and one after a meal or snack not containing bread. Though technically a series of blessings, *birkat hamazon* takes on the form of prayers that are typically read silently for ordinary meals, and often sung or chanted for special meals such as Shabbat, festivals, and special occasions. *Birkat hamazon* can be found in almost all prayer books and is often printed in a variety of artistic styles in a small booklet called a *birchon*.

TABLE 4.1

All of These Blessings Begin with the Phrase, "Blessed Are You, God, King of the Universe" (*Baruch ata adonai eloheinu melech haolam*)

Before eating bread (bread symbolizes all food, so if this blessing is said, no others are needed)	who brings forth bread from the ground	*Hamotzi lehem min ha'aretz*
Before eating foods (other than bread) made from wheat, barley, oats, rye, or spelt such as cake, cookies, cereals, crackers, pies and pastry	who creates species of nourishment	*Borei minei mezonot*
Before drinking wine or grape juice	who creates the fruit of the vine	*Borei p'ri ha gafen*
Before eating tree-grown fruit	who creates the fruit of the tree	*Borei p'ri ha eytz*
Before eating produce that grew directly from the earth, such as potatoes or carrots	who creates the fruit of the ground	*Borei p'ri ha adama*
Before eating or drinking other foods	through whose word everything came to be	*She-ha-kol n'hiyeh bidvaro*

The scriptural source for the requirement to say *birkat hamazon* is, "When you have eaten and are satisfied, you shall bless the Lord, your God for the good land which he gave you" (Deuteronomy 8:10). *Birkat hamazon* is made up of four blessings. The first blessing is a blessing of thanks for the food, the second a blessing of thanks for the land of Israel, the third concerns Jerusalem, and the fourth thanks God for his goodness. After these four blessings are a series of short prayers, each beginning with the word *harachaman* (The merciful one), which ask for God's compassion. The blessing said after non-bread meals or snacks is called *bracha achrona* and is a shorter blessing with the same themes as *birkat hamazon*.

There are many other laws regarding *birkat hamazon*. One should wait less than 40 minutes after completing the meal to recite the *birkat*. Additionally, it is customary for people to recite *birkat* in the exact location in which they ate. There is a call to prayer at the beginning of *birkat* that necessitates at least 3, preferably 10, people. Orthodox Jews only count men in these numbers and will leave out the call to prayer if there are less than 3 men present.

JEWISH, KOSHER, KOSHER-STYLE, ETHNIC, AND KOSHER ETHNIC MEALS

Judaism is both a religion and a cultural identity. Even the most observant of American Jews are influenced by American and international foods and strive to include dishes from those cuisines in their daily and holiday meals. There are also culturally Jewish meals that have been adopted by mainstream America. Before discussing these variations, the differences in Jewish food, kosher food, kosher-style food, ethnic food, and kosher ethnic food within American Jewry are discussed.

Jewish food is food that has a cultural association with Judaism from throughout the Diaspora. Because many Jews keep kosher, it is often kosher or kosher-style but can be prepared outside of the dietary laws as well. In New York City many iconic foods such as bagels and lox; corned beef on rye sandwiches; New York cheesecake; knishes, a mashed potato-filled savory pastry; and egg cream, a milk, seltzer, and syrup mock milkshake containing neither egg nor cream, are ethnic Jewish foods that are enjoyed by New Yorkers, tourists, and Americans outside of New York City. Similarly, falafel, fried balls of pureed chick peas served on pita bread, is an Israeli dish that can be found throughout the United States. These foods have strong associations with Jewish people and may or may not be kosher. For example, many delis serve both corned beef sandwiches and cheesecake or egg creams, a mixing of meat and dairy in violation of kosher laws, but still a culturally Jewish experience.

Egg Cream

1 oz. chocolate syrup   1/2 c. milk
3/4 c. seltzer

Combine syrup and milk in the bottom of a tall glass. Aggressively add seltzer while stirring with a long spoon.

Falafel

1 16 oz. can of chickpeas or   2 TBSP flour
  garbanzo beans, drained   1 small green chili, chopped
1 tsp ground coriander   salt and pepper to taste
1 onion, chopped   1/2 bunch fresh parsley
1 tsp ground cumin   leaves
3 cloves of garlic, chopped   oil for frying

Pulse ingredients in a food processor until a thick paste is formed. Mold into balls, about the size of ping pong balls. Fry at 350 degrees until golden brown (5–7 minutes). Serve hot in a pita with hummus, tahini (sesame paste), lettuce, tomato, and/or onion.

Kosher foods may or may not be culturally Jewish but do conform to the Jewish dietary laws. So a beef brisket with tzimmes, a sweet carrot and raisin dish traditionally served on Rosh Hashanah, is a Jewish food and can be prepared according to kosher dietary laws using kosher meat. Spaghetti bolognese, spaghetti with a meat sauce, is an Italian dish. However, by using kosher ingredients, not adding parmesan cheese, milk, or cream and observing other laws, this Italian dish could be made kosher.

Kosher-style is a designation often used by restaurants rather than home cooks. Foods prepared kosher-style are cooked in observance of the major dietary laws, such as not combining meat and dairy and avoiding pork, but may include some nonkosher ingredients and are made without the rabbinical supervision necessary for kosher food-service establishments.

Jewish Americans enjoy the foods of Jews from throughout the Diaspora, including the Mediterranean, Eastern Europe, and Western Europe but also eat ethnic foods of other cultures including Chinese, Italian, Mexican, Thai, Greek, and many others. Observant Jews often adapt the foods of these other ethnic groups to be kosher by, for example, substituting soy cheeses for dairy cheese to make a dish of chicken parmesan or substituting kosher beef salami for roast pork in Chinese fried rice. By following dietary laws and substituting ingredients where necessary, many ethnic dishes can become kosher ethnic dishes.

ADAPTING FOODS

Kosher laws can be used to socially bond the Jewish community and separate them from the mainstream, reinforced eloquently by Shylock's words in Shakespeare's *Merchant of Venice* (Act I, Scene III):

I will buy with you, sell with you, talk with you,
walk with you, and so following, but I will not eat
with you, drink with you, nor pray with you.

But they can also restrict a longing among observant Jews to belong to and engage with mainstream American culture. While ersatz pepperoni pizza, bacon and eggs, or a cheeseburger made with soy meat or soy cheese may not be authentic from a culinary perspective it allows kosher Jews—especially teens—to connect with a mainstream American experience if they so desire.

Jews who keep kosher have found many ways to make whatever kinds of foods they want, even those that may traditionally be nonkosher, by using substitute ingredients. In this way kosher Jews are able to bring into their daily meals many foods enjoyed throughout the United States, which in turn come from regions across the world, from New Orleans gumbo, to New England chowder, to Seattle miso soup.

One of the most common things kosher cooks do to adapt foods is to use either fake dairy or fake meat products. In this way, mashed potatoes, normally made with butter and milk or cream, can be made with margarine and soy milk and enjoyed at a meat meal. Similarly, soy "meat" crumbles may be eaten with pasta and cheese to mimic the effect of bacon or meat while conforming to dietary laws. The soy and health food industry has advanced this style of kosher cooking in the last five years; however, there are also some substitute ingredients that are used in typical meals that have been around for many years.

Margarine is one of the most important substitutions that kosher Jews use to make certain foods more kosher-friendly. Nondairy margarine allows

Jewish cooks to make cakes, cookies, and other desserts nondairy, an important end to a meat meal, especially for holidays, as well as soups, sautés, breads, and anything else one may use butter for. Margarine tastes similar to butter and has the same properties, which means that it does not change the basic chemistry of recipes. Indeed, in addition to the cheaper cost of oleo-margarine, the Jewish market was a key factor in developing the demand for margarine in the United States.

There are also many traditional products that are substitutes for milk and cream. There are nondairy creamers that may be used in coffee or even whipped to create a nondairy whipped cream. There are also products that more closely resemble milk that may be used in any recipe that calls for milk. It is important to recognize, however, that the milk and cream replacements do not always taste like their dairy counterparts and can react poorly in baking recipes that rely heavily on certain chemical and physical attributes of the milk and cream. However, nondairy milk and cream products can be used in lasagnas, chicken dishes, or any number of other traditionally meat-based foods.

The growth of vegetarian and soy-based products in the United States has been very beneficial for kosher cooks. Nearly any vegetarian meal can easily be made kosher if cooked in a kosher kitchen. Soy milk and soy cheese are two common things used to make eating kosher easier. The possibility of eating a "cheeseburger" not only satisfies kosher Jews' stomachs, it also gives them the ability to feel more a part of mainstream American food culture.

Nonmeat soup powders are frequently used in dairy soups and other dishes requiring stock, and the advent of products such as soy bacon and sausage, mock pork and shrimp, meat crumbles, and other soy-meat products has allowed kosher Jews to safely explore the forbidden and to create some delicious everyday meals in the process.

The other category of adaptations to food that Jews explore on a daily basis relates to ethnic foods. As any other Americans, especially those living in or near cities with abundant ethnic cuisine, Jews are curious about food from other regions and countries and attempt to adapt those foods to be kosher. Jewish Americans have an affinity toward Chinese food in particular, evidenced by the large number of Kosher Chinese products such as marinades, noodles, and sauces, and even Chinese restaurants.[1] Sociologists Gaye Tuchman and Harry Levine in an article "New York Jews and Chinese Food: The Social Construction of an Ethnic Pattern," identify a variety of factors for this connection, including geographical proximity among immigrants, similar food products such as cabbage, onions, and garlic, the absence of dairy from meat meals, similarly non-Christian calendars, and a lack of Christian iconography in the restaurants, unlike other ethnic eateries like Italian and Greek. It is not uncommon for a kosher Jew to make a Chinese food dinner of chicken with broccoli or pepper steak. Although dishes like pork fried rice or shrimp lo mein are clearly off-limits, kosher chefs find ways to make Chinese food their own by using substitute products like imitation shrimp or by using kosher ingredients in classic Chinese and Chinese American dishes.

In addition to Chinese food, kosher chefs find ways to make many other cuisines agreeable to the laws of kashrut. Although Mexican food in America usually necessitates meat and cheese being eaten together, kosher chefs get around this either by using soy meat or soy cheese. Additionally, Jewish American chefs also make Italian food and will simply leave out the cheese when making things like spaghetti and meatballs or will make chicken parmesan with soy cutlets or soy cheese to replace either the meat or the cheese. Indian food may easily be adapted to kosher cooking by substituting soy milk or non-dairy creamer in any recipes that call for milk and meat together, and all forms of American regional cuisine can be enjoyed as long as there are substitutes for nonkosher meats and dairy. As Marcie Cohen Ferris documents in her book *Matzoh Ball Gumbo*, there is even a Jewish tradition of southern barbecue using beef instead of pork.[2] By adapting ethnic foods to be kosher, American Jews are participating in the same process in which all other Americans participate; they blend their own cultural traditions with the rich immigrant history of the United States and adapt and cook accordingly.

MEAT MEALS

Jewish Americans who keep kosher often only eat one meat meal a day due to the necessary waiting period of six hours after a meat meal and to the prohibition on combining meat and dairy. It is for these reasons that Jewish Americans rarely, if ever, have a meat breakfast. Aside from the natural concern of which meats one would eat at breakfast that are kosher—bacon, pork sausage, and ham clearly off-limits—eating a meat breakfast would mean not eating other common American breakfast foods, such as cereal and milk, pastries, pancakes, waffles, and yogurt, foods that are dairy or rely heavily on dairy ingredients. Due to the growing trend of kosher products mirroring those found in the nonkosher world, there are some companies that now make beef breakfast sausages. However, it is more common to have a mock-meat breakfast with soy bacon and other meatless meat products or simply pastries and fruit, hot or cold cereal, bagels with lox, or eggs, which are appropriate for either meat or dairy meals.

Meat lunches are much more common than meat breakfasts. Because delicatessen cold cuts are such popular Jewish American foods, many people who keep kosher eat deli sandwiches for lunch. In major cities there are kosher delis that make overstuffed meat sandwiches with homemade turkey, roast beef, corned beef, pastrami, salami, bologna, liverwurst, or tongue. There is often much care taken in the preparation of these deli meats. Kosher corned beef is typically made with brisket and is brined with salt, sugar, bay leaves, pepper, and other herbs, cured in the refrigerator, and then simmered in water on the stovetop.

Corned Beef

The number 18, *chai* in Hebrew, is symbolic of life in Jewish tradition.

1 beef brisket, about 7–8 pounds

Brine

7 qts. water, warm enough to dissolve salt	1 bay leaf
18 peppercorns, crushed	18 cloves garlic, peeled
3 c. kosher salt (approximately)	1 tsp dried thyme
	18 cloves
	1/2 tsp saltpeter

Prepare brine in large nonreactive pot by mixing all ingredients. Soak brisket in brine for one week, turning occasionally, weighted down to submerge.

Rinse and simmer in fresh water until tender, about 3 hours.

Kosher corned beef may be heavily seasoned with black pepper and other spices to make pastrami or barbeque pastrami, depending on the seasonings used. Roast or smoked turkey and roast beef are also common and are made in the usual roasting or smoking fashion. Liverwurst is a liver lunchmeat made of chopped livers and seasonings. Finally, tongue is made by brining and hot smoking a beef tongue and slicing it very thinly.

These sandwiches are commonly eaten on rye bread and are accompanied by pickles and coleslaw and a spicy mustard, mayonnaise, or Russian dressing. People who wish to make these sandwiches at home often buy the meat and bread at a local deli and assemble the sandwiches themselves, or they buy prepackaged kosher turkey or other meats and breads. There are a myriad of variations on a deli sandwich. It may be eaten hot or cold, on a challah roll, a Kaiser roll, or pumpernickel bread, with half sour pickles instead of sour pickles, and accompanied by potato salad, potato chips, lettuce, tomato, French fries, and many other things. School children bring deli sandwiches with them as bagged lunches, and business men and women bring them to work.

There are other meat lunches that American Jews often enjoy; however, these are similar to the meals that any other American may eat, with accommodations for the laws of kashrut if necessary.

It is extremely rare for American Jews who keep kosher to have meat snacks. There are a number of reasons for this. First, it is because there are simply few kosher meat snacks on the market. Also, it does not seem worthwhile to most who keep kosher to eat a small snack of meat and then have to wait three to six hours to eat anything dairy. People who are kosher often assess their meal or food by thinking about future meals and snacks and weighing whether or not it is worth it to "be *fleishig*" (to eat a meat meal) and not be able to eat any milk products for the ensuing hours.

If there is one meal that is most commonly a meat meal for American Jews who keep kosher, it is dinner. As is customary in general American culinary culture, dinner is viewed as the largest meal of the day and as a time for the family to come together, if schedules permit, to enjoy a nice meal together. Those who are kosher perceive meat as a fancier and more formal food than anything one may make with dairy products and therefore often reserve eating meat for dinner time. The fact that there is no meal following dinner makes it very easy to avoid dairy products in the six hours following dinner. Although not as much care is put into the preparation of a weekday meat meal as is put into the preparation of a Shabbat meat meal, it is still common to eat meat during weeknights since meat is viewed as more substantial than other things. The actual meat that people may eat again varies regionally and is extremely similar to general American or ethnic foods, with the appropriate adaptations. Some sample typical weekday meals, as reported by our friends around the United States, are a Chinese fried rice with lamb and peas, grilled chicken and eggplant, spaghetti with meat sauce, beef tacos, steak and potatoes, and chicken and vegetable stew, representing a wide range of ethnic and mainstream American meals.

DAIRY MEALS

American Jews, especially those of Eastern European descent, tend to eat large amounts of dairy. It is important to note that when discussing Jewish food, dairy includes not only milk products but any nonmeat meal. So a tuna salad sandwich, while not containing any dairy, would be considered a dairy meal in conversation as it is not a meat meal.

Because of the problems already discussed with having a meat breakfast, those who keep kosher often have a dairy breakfast. The breakfast that American Jews eat, even the most observant and religious of American Jews, is no different from the type of breakfast that other Americans eat. There are a number of kosher cereals and other to-go breakfast foods such as granola bars and yogurts that people will eat when they are in a rush to get to school or work. On a more relaxing day people will make eggs, which most American Jews maintain do not need to be marked as kosher, bagels, often eaten with cream cheese and a hard-boiled egg or smoked or preserved fish, pancakes (there are kosher pancake and waffle mixes available), waffles, oatmeal, grits, biscuits, or other foods, depending on the region of the country in which they live, family traditions, and personal preference.

Lunch is a meal that can be either dairy or meat on a daily basis, depending on the mood and tastes of the individual. Children who are enrolled in Jewish schools or summer day camps are often required to bring a dairy kosher lunch to school so that there are no problems with meat and milk mixing in the lunchroom. These school children bring the same things that any other American students bring, as long as there is no meat involved: peanut butter and jelly, cheese sandwiches, bagel with cream cheese, egg salad sandwich, cookies, chips, fruit, and so on. Other dairy lunches that people may eat are again the same as the lunches that other Americans eat. Dairy salads like tuna fish, sandwiches like eggplant parmesan, and soups like cream of broccoli are all common things for American Jews to enjoy for lunch. The traditional dairy foods such as kugels and blintzes are usually reserved for special occasions and are not eaten for an everyday lunch unless purchased from a dairy restaurant.

Dairy dinners are just as common to eat during the week as are meat dinners. Italian food is a favorite among many Jewish Americans, and many people have pasta dishes, lasagnas, or casseroles for dinner. Just as with other Americans, especially working Americans, American Jews are often in a time crunch when it comes to weeknight dinners and make things that are quick and easy. There are many kosher frozen and preprepared meals that have become popular mainstays on the shelves of Jewish supermarkets. However, dinner is often a challenging meal for the kosher cook who does not wish to eat these heavily processed foods. There are many regional variations that come into play with dinner. Those living on the West Coast may make a California cuisine dinner of avocado, goat cheese, and fig salad, while those living in the Southwest may make vegetable quesadillas, and those living in the South may make fried chicken and biscuits. A look on the family dinner table of most of the United States would be very similar to the Jewish American table. An informal survey of our friends nationwide tells us that cheese pizza, grilled salmon with rice, fish parmesan, mushroom and cheese quiche, and vegetable lasagna are all typical dairy meals.

NONKOSHER TYPICAL MEALS

Most American Jews do not keep kosher. In fact, only around 20 percent of American Jews keep some version of kashrut in the home.[3] However, this does not mean that they do not follow the similar patterns for typical meals that other kosher American Jews and other Americans follow. While many Jewish Americans do not keep strict kosher, many do not allow pork or shell-fish in the home and many others find themselves avoiding mixing meat and dairy, as much for cultural or traditional reasons as for religious reasons. Many Jewish American adults grew up in kosher homes and, while they may relax some rules as adults, eating shellfish in restaurants, for example, may not have developed a taste for pork, cheeseburgers, or other nonkosher foods. Conversely, there are many American Jews who identify themselves as cul-tural Jews or Reform Jews and wholly disregard the kosher laws, even eating pork barbecue or bacon. Finally, many American Jews maintain a kosher or kosher-style home but allow themselves to eat nonkosher food in restaurants or in the homes of non-Jews.

Regardless of kashrut, it is common for even nonobservant and nonaffili-ated Jews to enjoy bagels and lox or other smoked fish for breakfast. Although this is a special occasion breakfast for some, if there is any breakfast that Jews tend to eat during the week it is this.

There are a variety of components that make up this meal, and it is note-worthy that the home cook rarely makes bagels, lox, or cream cheese from scratch. Most people buy these things from bagel bakeries or supermarkets. The "appetizing store" is a Jewish phenomenon that developed in the cities of the northeastern United States. These stores carry the fixings for these types of meals, including smoked and cured salmon (lox), pickled and preserved herring, specialty cheeses, pickles, and sweets. The bagels themselves are cus-tomarily plain or flavored with dried savory spices and seeds, such as onion, garlic, poppy seeds, or sesame seeds. People have different preferences for the consistency and taste of their bagels. While some prefer a hard crust and soft center, others prefer an all-around chewy bagel.

Lox or smoked salmon may be prepared in many different ways, and al-though some attempt to make it at home with home-smokers, most buy it from a supermarket or appetizing store. Basic cured salmon, lox, from the Scandinavian *gravlax,* is a side of salmon cured with salt, sometimes dill, sugar, or other spices. This cured salmon can then be smoked using a variety of types of wood to make a wide variety of smoked salmon. Herring is another traditional Jewish appetizing fish and is cured in a liquid brine of salt, sugar, and water. Other herbs and spices may be added to alter the flavor. The bagel and preserved fish is combined with some combination of cream cheese, on-ions, capers, cucumber, tomato, and olives.

The deli lunch that nonkosher American Jews may enjoy is similar to the lunches that kosher Jews enjoy. However, nonkosher Jews do not necessarily eat any more of a variety of foods for lunch (or for any other meal) than do kosher Jews or average Americans. Those Jewish Americans who do not keep kosher frequently add cheese or other nonkosher products to their deli sandwiches. One common sandwich is the reuben, which is built of corned beef, melted Swiss cheese, and Russian dressing. While this is a Jewish-style sandwich, it is definitely not kosher. Jews who do not keep kosher obviously may eat nonkosher meats alongside their deli meats; however, some may avoid doing so. Even kosher-style nonkosher delis do not customarily serve pig or shellfish products.

Finally, dinner and other snacks for this set of Jewish Americans is closely aligned to the foods that other Americans eat on a normal basis, obviously taking into account regional variations. Some nonkosher American Jewish tables will look identical to those of non-Jews, including even barbecued pork ribs, shrimp gumbo, or beef stroganoff. Others will make small adaptations to use kosher-style recipes, substituting turkey or beef sausage for pork in an Italian pasta dish or flaked fish for crab in crabcakes without fully following kosher laws.

BEVERAGES AND DESSERTS

Like most Americans, a variety of beverages such as water, milk, juice, soda, beer, wine, tea or coffee may all make an appearance at the American Jewish table. Jews do drink alcohol, especially wine on the Sabbath and other holidays. Whiskey and schnapps are also popular, though more typically before or after meals rather than at the table. For kosher Jews, beverages must also conform to kosher laws. That is, milk, cream in coffee and other dairy beverages would only be drunk at a dairy meal for a kosher Jew. At a meat meal no milk would be drunk and nondairy creamer used in hot beverages.

Desserts too resemble those of the American table in general. Ice cream, canned or fresh fruit, fruit compote or salad, cakes, pies, cookies, or other baked goods may all appear on the American Jewish table. Dried fruit and nuts are also common finishes to a meal. As with beverages, for Jews who keep kosher, the dessert, if dairy, must follow a dairy meal, and if following a meat meal must be pareve (neither meat nor dairy). Ensuring that baked goods contain no butter, milk, or other dairy is especially important since these are such common ingredients.

A number of nondairy items used in desserts such as soy or rice milk, soy-based ice cream, nondairy creamer and pareve puddings are available for kosher Jews who wish to have the approximation of a dairy item at a meat meal.

NOTES

1. "Kosherfest: The Business of Kosher Food and Beverage" (December 2006), http://Kosherfest.com.

2. Marcie Cohen Ferris, *Matzoh Ball Gumbo: Culinary Tales of the Jewish South* (Chapel Hill, NC: University of North Carolina Press, 2005).

3. Gaye Tuchman and Harry Gene Levine, "New York Jews and Chinese Food: The Social Construction of an Ethnic Pattern," in *The Taste of American Place*, ed. Shortridge and Shortridge (New York: Rowman and Littlefield, 1998), pp. 163–200.

5

Eating Out

Dining in restaurants for Jewish Americans is common and is made possible by the increasing number of kosher, vegetarian, kosher-style, and Jewish restaurants, in addition to ethnic, regional, and other establishments. The type of restaurant that a Jewish person will eat at or take out from is largely dependent on her or his level of adherence to kashrut and cultural conventions. Consequently, there are some Jews who will eat anything anywhere, some who will dine at a nonkosher restaurant but will closely restrict their menu options to fish or vegetarian items to avoid nonkosher meat, and still others who will only dine out at rabbinically supervised kosher establishments. Depending on location, finding a kosher, vegetarian, kosher-style, or Jewish restaurant can be difficult. Although these types of restaurants are common in major cities, rural and suburban areas can present challenges for a Jewish diner.

KOSHER ESTABLISHMENTS

Just as food products need to be certified kosher, so too do kosher restaurants need to be certified kosher. Certification typically involves one or more visits by a rabbi, often a member of a rabbinical group, who evaluates the menu, the products in house, and the recipes to ensure their adherence to the kosher laws. The rabbi may make periodic inspection visits and, after an infraction, may have to make the kitchen kosher again, a process that involves cleaning, prayers, and symbolic acts.

Upon certification, the restaurant may advertise and post prominently that they are operating under rabbinical supervision by the authority of a certain rabbinical group or individual rabbi. Deciding which marks of approval to accept is up to each individual Jewish diner, especially since different rabbis will often have different standards by which to measure the kashrut of the restaurants. For example, "Under the supervision of Rabbi Jon," may not be sufficient for observant Jews, whereas "Under the supervision of Rabbi Jon and the Union of Orthodox Jewish Congregations" gives the certification more authority.

When evaluating a food establishment for kosher certification, one major determining factor of whether or not a restaurant will be certified is whether or not it is open on Shabbat. Many rabbis will not certify that a restaurant is kosher even if it meets all of the culinary and law standards if it is open on Shabbat. However, other more liberal rabbis will certify that the restaurant is kosher every day but Saturday.

Any restaurant that is certified kosher has what is called a *mashgiach*, a special type or rabbi or trained rabbinical appointee. It is this person's job to check that the kitchen and dining areas of the restaurant all uphold the laws of kashrut. In most kosher restaurants this is a full-time job that requires much attentiveness. Restaurants wishing to hold to the highest standards of kashrut employ a full-time *mashgiach*. Although this person may fulfill other roles in the restaurant, it is this person's primary job to make sure that all of the food preparation is acceptable. This type of *mashgiach* is called a *mashgiach tamidit*, which specifically means a *mashgiach* who is there all the time. It is necessary to have the *mashgiach* there all the time because there are shipments, menus, and differing food preparations that must always be checked. In addition, many kosher restaurants employ cooks and other personnel of many religions, so the *mashgiach* plays an important role in training non-Jewish employees in the laws of kashrut and ensuring that those new to their understanding of the law do not make any errors that could put the restaurant in violation of kashrut. Often, though, the manager or owner of the restaurant fills the role, with occasional supplementary visits from the actual *mashgiach*. Although these restaurants are also considered kosher, they are perhaps held to a lower standard and are therefore not frequented by the most observant of American Jews.

There are many responsibilities that a *mashgiach* has in a restaurant, and these responsibilities differ based upon how strictly kosher the *mashgiach* and the *mashgiach*'s organization are. In all kosher restaurants the *mashgiach* is in charge of checking shipments for any possible problems. The *mashgiach* checks that all products being used are marked as kosher, and if necessary, nondairy. The *mashgiach* is also responsible for ensuring that no one brings any outside food into the restaurant or the kitchen, even if it is supposedly kosher, because it can potentially compromise the kashrut of the restaurant. The *mashgiach* is in charge of checking produce for bugs in establishments that hold that all fruits and vegetables must be thoroughly cleaned for all bugs, lest they make the food nonkosher (bugs are not kosher to eat, even if accidentally consumed). Also, because liver is particularly difficult to make kosher, the *mashgiach* is often in charge of preparing at least part of any liver dishes that restaurants serve. In some establishments it is the *mashgiach's* job to turn on the ovens. That way, even if non-Jewish cooks are employed in the restaurant, the *mashgiach* "cooks" by lighting the oven. This is a symbolic response to a medieval prohibition against non-Jews cooking kosher food for Jews. In this period there were many theological wars between Jews and non-Jews involving the laws of the bible and the necessity to follow them. It was for this cultural reason that Jews did not trust non-Jews to cook their food.

There is also a type of *mashgiach* that visits factories and is called a *mashgiach nichnas v'yotzei*, or a *mashgiach* who goes in and out. Factories do not need a full-time *mashgiach* because they are automated and any actions that they take with the food are generally unchanging. However, if a factory changes part of the process of how they make their product, or if they change any one of the ingredients, they must notify their *mashgiach*. A *mashgiach nichnas v'yotzei* generally only visits the factories for which he or she (usually a he) is responsible a few times a year.

The politics of *mashgiachs* and the organizations of which *mashgiachs* are a part can be very interesting. While many *mashgiachs* are associated with organizations such as the Orthodox Union (known commonly as OU), which have a specific trademarked mark of kashrut, many other *mashgiachs* are individuals (generally rabbis) with their own seal of approval. Depending upon the level of kashrut one observes, these unassociated individuals may not carry enough weight to be considered kosher. In very observant communities people defer to their rabbi to tell them which *mashgiachs* are acceptable and which are not.

There are a number of reasons that people are more suspicious of *mashgiachs* who are on their own than *mashgiachs* who are associated with a particular organization. If, for example, a restaurant is certified by the OU as kosher, then the Orthodox Union has helped the restaurant find a *mashgiach* who is held to a particular set of standards and who is employed by the OU. This means that the OU pays the *mashgiach*, not the restaurant. When a *mashgiach* is unaffiliated his standards are not supervised by a certifying organization. Also, there is more of a possibility for underhanded dealings and bribes, since the restaurant would be paying the *mashgiach* directly. The restaurant, for example, could bribe the *mashgiach* to allow nonkosher food, or even could withhold pay if the *mashgiach* does not allow certain questionable ingredients.

Often when a rabbi tells the members of his community that a certain restaurant with an unaffiliated *mashgiach* is kosher, the rabbi is basing his opinion on friendships, political or familial ties, and even possible financial gain.

There are very few differences between the *mashgiach's* role in meat and dairy restaurants. The only added difficulty with meat restaurants is that the *mashgiach* must be even more aware of the ingredients that the kitchen is using, because there it is common to find dairy ingredients hidden in certain products. The other added difficulty with meat restaurants is the issue of fish. Although fish and meat can be eaten at the same meal, they cannot be cooked in the same place or eaten with the same utensils. It is for this reason that meat restaurants wishing to serve fish often have a separate preparation and cooking area for the fish.

Kosher restaurants only exist in areas with a sizable observant Jewish population. Though there are some smaller suburban and rural areas of the country that are home to considerable numbers of observant Jews, most of the Jews in this country who observe kashrut live in or around major cities. In smaller towns with small Jewish populations it may be that there are insufficient numbers of observant Jews to support any kosher restaurants. In that situation, an enterprising restaurateur may open a kosher delicatessen or vegetarian restaurant designed to appeal to Jews and non-Jews alike. Conversely, in large cities, many establishments may have kosher certification so as to be inclusive of more diners. For example, in New York City, many of the national brand doughnut/fast food shops like Dunkin Donuts are certified kosher, serving no meat on breakfast sandwiches, so they can appeal to kosher Jews, halal Muslims, and others. It is simply good business.

Kosher restaurants are placed into two categories, meat or dairy. Since meat and dairy need to be separate at meals, it follows that they need to be separate in restaurants and even cooked in separate kitchens. Often, however, popular kosher restaurants open two sides or two locations in order to boost business and clientele.

As discussed elsewhere, kosher restaurants may serve food that is culturally Jewish. Or they may not. It is possible to adhere to kosher laws and cook food from many world cultures. So when appealing to a kosher clientele, it is good business to serve more than just Jewish food. Just as other Americans enjoy food from around the world, so too do Jewish Americans. There are kosher restaurants that have cuisine based in all ethnicities and cultures. Japanese, Mexican, French, Indian, Italian, Jewish, Russian, Polish, Chinese, Thai, and South American foods are all featured in both meat and dairy restaurants. While some kosher restaurants are popular only with those who keep kosher, there are other establishments that cater to kosher Jews, nonkosher Jews, and non-Jews. Many Muslims patronize kosher establishments, because both religions prohibit pork. If a restaurant is kosher, a Muslim diner can be assured that no pork is present. Further, many people associate kashrut with cleanliness and health. Consequently, people from many religions report selecting kosher restaurants and food products for reasons that have little to do with religious observance.

Many of the types of restaurants that exist in most of America exist in kosher form. There are expensive restaurants with impressive architectural and interior design serving innovative cuisine sought after by Jews and non-Jews alike. And there are quick dingy pizza joints and sandwich shops. There are a number of various guides, both on the Internet and in print, that list kosher restaurants and the type of kosher certification that they have.

VEGETARIAN RESTAURANTS

Jews who keep kosher but are not insistent that all of the food they eat be marked with a symbol of kashrut often will eat in strictly vegetarian (or in some cases only vegan) restaurants. Although there is always the possibility that a worker is enjoying a ham and cheese sandwich in the back of the kitchen, many people are willing to overlook that slim possibility in order to enjoy a relaxing meal out, especially in those places that have few or no kosher restaurants, such as small towns or when traveling abroad in predominantly non-Jewish areas.

As vegetarian restaurants become more popular and common, more Jews are experimenting with vegetarian cuisine. Although Jews certainly have a special and strong relationship with meat, the boon of vegetarian cuisine has opened up many people's eyes to meat substitutes such as seitan, soy, and tempeh. There are those who will only eat in vegan restaurants, because of some of the kashrut issues with cheese and dairy products (some people will only eat cheese that has been specially marked above the normal kosher symbol, which is called *cholev yisroel*) and also those who will only order vegan dishes in a vegetarian restaurant.

Eating in vegetarian restaurants has become quite acceptable in some kashrut-observant circles. Men who cover their head with a *kippa,* a yarmulke or head covering, regularly but eat in nonkosher restaurants remove their *kippa* upon entering the restaurant. However, it has become commonplace to see men wearing their *kippa* in vegetarian restaurants. Also, many synagogues and other Jewish organizations ask vegetarian restaurants to cater events or meetings. Vegetarian restaurants often advertise in the newsletters and on the bulletin boards of Jewish organizations, and it is common for kosher cooks to buy cookbooks from popular vegetarian establishments.

KOSHER-STYLE RESTAURANTS

In addition to actual certified kosher restaurants, many establishments are kosher-style restaurants. These places, which are common all over the country, are not meant to attract kosher Jews. Rather, they are meant to attract Jews who have a strong cultural connection to Jewish and cultural food but who do not observe the kosher laws, as well as non-Jews who enjoy culturally Jewish food. Kosher-style restaurants, like the famous Carnegie Deli in New York, or the famous Canter's Fairfax Deli in Los Angeles, would not necessarily appear to an uninformed observer to be any different from restaurants that are kosher.

Kosher-style restaurants do not usually serve foods that are inherently non-kosher, like pork products or seafood. While some serve milk and meat in the same restaurant, they are not commonly combined in the same dish. For example, a kosher-style restaurant would never serve a cheeseburger; however, they may serve a knish, a potato pocket encased in pastry dough and baked, made with milk or cream, alongside a sandwich.

Kosher-style restaurants often serve meat that is marked with a kosher symbol. This is part of the allure of kosher-style restaurants. Chefs and restaurateurs wish to remind their diners of the wonderful kosher foods without necessarily being bound to all of the laws of kashrut. Many reform and nonobservant Jewish organizations will use kosher-style restaurants as caterers, and it is not unusual to find these restaurants crowded on Saturdays, since those who eat there are not necessarily observant but wish to do something to mark their Judaism on Shabbat.

NOT EATING OUT

There are many people who simply do not eat at any restaurant other than one that is marked as kosher, and still others who will only eat at restaurants with specific kashrut marks. Although this is rarely an ordeal for those living in places like New York, Chicago, Boston, or Los Angeles, this can certainly be problematic for those living in other parts of the country.

Never eating out in restaurants has many ramifications. First, it can clearly put a stress on whoever in the home is in charge of preparing the meals. Without the option of ordering a pizza or grabbing a quick Chinese food meal at the local restaurant, home cooks have the challenge of making every single meal at home with little to no help from prepared foods. Also, not eating out in any restaurants except ones that are kosher can be socially isolating. Many people are in social circles in which there are varying levels of kashrut observed, and while friends and family members may be understanding, there can still be some social difficulties and awkwardness with getting around this issue. Imagine being the only one of a group of school friends who could not go out with the rest of the crowd.

Of course, not eating out has other positive ramifications. The family or individuals spend less money on food and are able to spend more time at home together.

HOT DAIRY AND OTHER CONSIDERATIONS

There are many kosher consumers, especially those who identify with Conservative and Reform ideologies, who are willing to eat out in nonkosher restaurants, but who will only eat what is referred to as "hot dairy." This basically means that many of those people who keep kosher at home are willing to eat out in nonkosher restaurants, as long as they are not eating any meat products. Jews that eat hot dairy out, however, must still be careful about what they order. Just like strict vegetarians, Jews who keep this type of kashrut need to ensure that none of their foods have any hidden meats in them, specifically in any stocks that have been used to prepare vegetables or starches. It should also be noted that there are those who are willing to eat hot food out but will not eat anything made with cheese, because of the animal rennet found in many cheeses.

Such diners often maintain a kosher home and are active in the secular community. Therefore, they hold themselves to different standards when engaging with the community so that they can, say, attend a business dinner with people of various faiths.

There are also some people, usually more observant Conservative and some Orthodox Jews, who are willing to eat out in nonkosher restaurants as long as they are eating dairy food that is cold and has never been cooked. This may include salads, some types of sandwiches, desserts, and in some cases, foods like sushi. This line that people draw for themselves can sometimes be a difficult one to see. Although bread has been cooked, most people who eat only cold dairy out will eat bread or other pastry products, because it is highly unlikely that they would ever come near any meat. It is also important to recognize that while people may eat cold dairy out, that does not mean that they would take that food into their homes.

There are also many Jews who keep kosher in the home and keep only a version of kashrut when they go out to eat. For example, some people may be willing to eat meat out, but never combine it with dairy products, while others are willing to eat meat and cheese but would never touch shellfish or pork. The reason for these confusing eating patterns is that many Jews make an effort to keep a kosher home as a symbol of their faith just as much as a marker of their belief, and so they are willing to be more lenient when they are eating out. Because Jews are a minority in the United States, and, indeed, throughout the Diaspora, there is a continuum of tradition and assimilation that ranges from completely secular and assimilated, to kosher at home but not as strict when engaging with the secular community, to strictly kosher at all times. As discussed elsewhere in this book, there are many ideas about what it is to be an American Jew.

The tension between what people think is acceptable to eat out and what they think is acceptable to eat in their homes makes an interesting issue of taking out food and getting delivery. While some people who keep a kosher home and are willing to eat hot dairy out are willing to order in nonkosher food and eat it either with paper goods or on their actual dishes, other will only get take-out or delivery from kosher restaurants. It is uncommon, however, for someone who keeps a kosher home to bring nonkosher meat or shellfish into their house.

TRAVELING

For those Jews who keep kosher outside of their home, eating well can be especially challenging when traveling. Although it is becoming more common for airports, train stations, and bus stations to have vegetarian options, most have very few, and a kosher restaurant at an airport or train station is a rare sight. Most people who keep kosher have to scrounge in these places for kosher food. This becomes even more difficult for kosher consumers who are also nutrition-minded. It is not uncommon for someone to make a meal of a bag of potato chips, a piece of fruit, and a container of cookies while traveling since many packaged foods and uncut fruits and vegetables are kosher. Those who are willing to eat hot dairy out tend to get more creative and get things like french fries or a cheeseburger with all of the fixings but without the meat. Kosher Jews have a tendency to bring large amounts of food with them to ensure that they are well-fed throughout any trip, whether it be a two-hour car trip, or an overnight flight. For a kosher Jew who brings her or his meal along, a flight delay or other unexpected travel incident can be very challenging.

It is not uncommon for Jews to pack sandwiches for events like baseball games or trips to a local lake, since there are so few kosher options at these destinations. Once at a destination, the most strictly kosher Jews will occasionally order vacuum-packed heated kosher meals to enjoy, while others will only travel to specific kosher (or kosher-friendly) resorts.

NONRELIGIOUS JEWS

Nonreligious Jews eat out in the same way that many other non-Jewish Americans eat out in restaurants. While they may be more likely to attend kosher-style or Jewish cuisine restaurants, nonreligious Jews are just as likely to eat at a seafood restaurant or a local pizza place as any other American. Like many Americans, Jews love the cuisine of the world, and nonreligious Jews will dine at a wide variety of ethnic restaurants. In fact, the connection between Jewish Americans and Chinese restaurants is well documented both in popular culture and in scholarly literature. Jews love many types of food but especially Chinese food, and in large cities both nonkosher and kosher

Chinese restaurants abound. Nonreligious Jews are more likely to eat in kosher restaurants than the average American, especially on Passover.

There are some nonreligious Jews that make it a practice to always eat out (or get take-out/delivery) on Friday nights. This is their way of marking the Sabbath with a special meal, even if it is done so with nonkosher food. Conversely, there are many nonreligious American Jews who will eat out on any night of the week *except* for the Sabbath, when they insist on having a home-cooked family meal, often of traditional Jewish food. In many households, Sunday nights are marked by Chinese take-out food, the end of the only free weekend day for American Jews who work Monday through Friday and go to synagogue and celebrate the Sabbath on Saturday.

CATERING

The world of Jewish catering is vast and remarkable. Most major American cities or even small towns have access to a kosher caterer. Since caterers travel, unlike restaurants, a small town that cannot support a kosher restaurant can usually get a kosher caterer to travel in for business. Kosher caterers are used for baby namings and circumcisions, weddings, funerals, bar and bat mitzvahs, kiddish luncheons (luncheons held after services), birthday parties, anniversary parties, and much more. Kosher caterers do not typically serve only Jewish food; as haute cuisine gains popularity in American mainstream culture, kosher caterers are stepping up their menus to include such delicacies as sushi, lamb chops, foie gras, caviar, and more. In some major cities there are also large popular catering companies that have a kosher caterer within their business in order to pull in the small yet eager and wealthy Jewish communities. Often synagogues and other organizations have contracts with caterers that stipulate that if anyone wants to hold an event at that particular synagogue they must use the synagogue's caterer. One caterer is often the exclusive caterer of a number of synagogues in any city. In cases in which there is no caterer in the immediate vicinity of the more remote Jewish communities, many large caterers are willing to travel or to ship food.

As previously noted, many reform Jewish events are catered by nonkosher or kosher-style caterers.

Catering and caterers represent a particular challenge for the observant American Jew who engages with the broader community. It is relatively easy for a kosher Jew to avoid going to a *treyf* (nonkosher) restaurant by choosing another option such as eating at home, choosing a kosher restaurant, buying kosher packaged foods, or compromising at a vegetarian restaurant or with a hot or cold dairy meal, depending on her or his level of observance. But imagine being invited to a wedding celebration or having to attend a funeral of a non-Jewish or nonkosher Jewish colleague, classmate, neighbor, or friend.

It is socially awkward not to eat at a wedding feast. It is equally awkward to bring food from home to eat on paper plates. And while a conscientious host would arrange for packaged heat-and-serve meals for kosher guests at a nonkosher event, many hosts do not know the laws of kashrut, the level of observance of the guest, or even that such an accommodation would need to be made.

PASSOVER

Eating out on Passover is relatively impossible for Jews living in most places around the country. However, there are two ways in which people are able to enjoy a night of respite from the endless cooking on the holiday. Some synagogues or other Jewish institutions offer a Passover restaurant that is usually a catered affair held in a social hall or other large meeting room. There is a flat fee for these Passover restaurants and they usually include a meat buffet with a wide variety of chicken, meat, soups, salads, side dishes, and desserts.

The other way that people are able to eat out on Passover is to go to actual kosher restaurants that become kosher for Passover (a stricter kind of kosher) over the holiday. These restaurants close a day or two before the holiday begins in order to prepare the kitchen for Passover, a process very similar to preparing the home for Passover (see Chapter 6, Special Occasions). Although they are only able to be open for the four short days in between the religious festival days at the beginning and end of the holiday, these restaurants do an enormous amount of business, primarily because there are so few options over Passover. Although restaurants that have a Chinese, Mexican, or Italian theme are unable to open because the rice and pasta base of those cuisines is inherently not kosher for Passover, other types of restaurants are able to open.

CONCLUSION

Just as there is diversity among American Jews there is diversity among dining options, from full participation in all the great eating establishments the world has to offer, to an elaborate series of rules and compromises, to near total avoidance of eating out altogether.

For observant Jews, eating out presents a series of challenges that can take a great deal of thought, research, and creativity. This no doubt contributes to the prominent role of food and talk about food in Jewish American culture.

6

Special Occasions

The Jewish calendar includes a variety of holidays, celebrations, and other momentous occasions that are strongly related to food and drink. With the exception of the major and minor fast days that exist throughout the calendar, each holiday and life-cycle event has at least one food that is heavily associated with it. For each holiday Jews make it a point to gather with family and loved ones to say the appropriate blessings and prayers for the occasion and to enjoy a feast together. Even on fast days, the absence of food and the food marking the beginning and end of the fast is significant. For those Jews who are not especially observant of the Jewish laws, the foods specific to each occasion may be their primary connection to the holiday.

All Jewish holidays and events are traditionally marked by a specific type of service, usually in a synagogue. The holidays follow the Jewish lunar calendar and start and end at sunset. The holidays vary in length from one day to many days, and because the lunar calendar operates independently of the Roman calendar, the dates according to the Roman calendar vary. In addition, for observant Jews the length of certain holidays such as Passover, Shavuot, and Sukkot, differs between Israel and the Diaspora. Passover, Shavuot, and Sukkot are the three pilgrimage harvest holidays and are each a week long. In Israel, the first and last days of these holidays are observed in a manner that requires more attention to Jewish law, prayer, and practice. In the Diaspora, however, these holidays have two significant days at the beginning at two at the end. The rabbis say that the reason for this goes back to the times of the Temple, before there was any efficient means of communication. Jews everywhere wanted to ensure that they were celebrating the holidays at the same time that those in Jerusalem were celebrating them. Although there are now accurate ways of telling when the sun has set in Jerusalem, traditional Jews preserve this practice by observing extra days of the holiday to mark that they live in the Diaspora and not in Israel. Reform Jews have returned to the practice of celebrating only one day of the holiday.

The observance of holidays in American Jewish culture varies. Most American Jews who belong to a synagogue or other organization attend services for the major holidays, and possibly during the weekly services for the Sabbath or for other favorite holidays. Those who are active in their denomination, whether Reform, Reconstructionist, Renewal, Conservative, Orthodox, or others, usually celebrate each holiday in some manner. Even those who do not wish to fulfill the commandments surrounding a holiday or attend synagogue will often prepare the foods that are customary to eat on that holiday. Parents who have children enrolled in Hebrew school or religious school usually mark holidays and life-cycle events more than others because their children are involved in the cultural and religious appreciation of the holidays in school.

THE JEWISH HOLIDAY CALENDAR

Jewish holidays may be separated into four groups. The pilgrimage holidays, Passover (Pesach), Shavuot, and Sukkot are all commanded by the Torah and were originally marked by a pilgrimage of the Jews into Jerusalem to the Temple for a special priestly service. The second set of holidays, commonly referred to as the High Holidays, are Rosh Hashana and Yom Kippur. These are considered the most holy and important days in the Jewish calendar. The third group of holidays, which includes Hanukkah, Purim, and Tu Bishvat, are not discussed in the Torah. Rather, the rabbis explain the commandments and customs of these holidays in the Talmud and other rabbinic writings. The weekly observance of the Sabbath (Shabbat) receives special mention and can be considered a category unto itself.

HOLIDAYS ACCORDING TO CALENDAR YEAR

Shabbat

Shabbat, or the Sabbath, is the Jewish day of rest and is observed each week from sundown on Friday until sundown on Saturday. It is the central part of the week for observant American Jews and is the means by which Jews understand and mark the passage of time. Preparation for Shabbat is taken very seriously and is begun early in the week with cooking, cleaning, and planning. The origin of the observance of Shabbat comes from Genesis 2, in which God created the world in six days and is said to have rested on the seventh day. It says, "And on the seventh day God finished His work which He had made; and He rested on the seventh day from all His work which He had made. And God blessed the seventh day, and hallowed it; because that in it He rested from all His work which God in creating had made" (Genesis 2:2). It is for this reason that Jews rest on Saturday, the seventh day of the week according to the Jewish calendar.

There are a variety of observances associated with Shabbat, and those who observe the laws of Shabbat are referred to as *shomer* Shabbat. The way in which people observe Shabbat is an indicator of the way in which they may observe other holidays, because the observance of Shabbat is similar in many ways to the observance of other major holidays. American Jews commonly pick and choose which Shabbat laws they wish to observe. As with everything in Judaism, there are varying levels and multiple ways of identifying with the traditions and variations of the rigor and interpretation in which laws are observed.

The central theme of Shabbat is rest. This idea leads to an assortment of negative commandments, or forbidden behaviors. On Shabbat Jews are not allowed to work or create in any way from sunset on Friday night until Saturday night at sunset. It follows that writing, making music, doing artwork, or any other form of creating or work is prohibited. It is also forbidden to make fire or to do anything that would make fire. This is interpreted in different ways. Some more observant Jews will not use any electricity, hot water, or stoves and ovens, because all of those activities involve creating fire. Others are willing to use electricity, because some rabbis argue that electricity is not creating a fire; rather, it is completing a current. Additionally, it is forbidden to travel on Shabbat. Although many Jews will travel to synagogue by car, most traditional Jews will not ride in a car or take a bike, roller blades, scooter, or other means of transportation to get anywhere. Observant Jews often walk to synagogue, and it is consequently important that they live within walking distance of a synagogue. Finally, it is prohibited to carry things on Shabbat. Since this is a particularly difficult prohibition, the rabbis in the Talmudic era established the idea of an *eiruv*, which is a designated area in which people are able to carry things.

Perhaps the most relevant prohibition on Shabbat here is the prohibition of cooking, which may seem odd considering the importance of food to the holiday. Cooking is not only creating and completing something, but it also involves lighting a fire. Traditional Jews will only warm food on Shabbat. Some use an oven that is at a low enough temperature to only warm, but not cook, while others use a hot plate. It is also common to use a stovetop device called a *blech*, which is a simple piece of sheet metal placed over a low flame. The inability to cook on Shabbat is surely a challenge for observant Jews;

however it has in many ways spurred a great deal of creativity and innovation in the kitchen, resulting in some delectable traditional Shabbat foods.

There is also an array of laws on Shabbat that are positive commandments, or behaviors that are necessary to complete on Shabbat. Attendance in synagogue and prayer is necessary, along with enjoying Shabbat and honoring it by doing a variety of things that may be perceived as special, including sharing meals and time with friends and family. It is also quite relevant to note that it is a commandment to eat three full meals on Shabbat, and no more or less.

Shabbat begins promptly at sundown, and, like all other major holidays, is marked with the lighting of candles and the recitation of a blessing. It is traditionally the woman's job to light the candles. Once the candles are lit, calm sets over the house and Shabbat is ready to begin. Two of the things that are commanded to bless and enjoy on Shabbat are wine and challah. A blessing over the wine (*kiddush*) is recited, traditionally by the man, and each person at the table takes a sip of the wine (or grape juice). There are some other songs and prayers that are recited, after which it is time to make the blessing over the bread, or challah. Challah is an eggy yeast bread that is commonly braided and then glazed with an egg wash. Occasionally raisins, poppy seeds, sesame seeds, or other seasonings are added.

Traditional challah. © J. Susan
Cole Stone.

Challah

(makes 2–3 loaves)

Many challah recipes have seven ingredients, a reference to the seventh day of the week (the Sabbath) on which it is eaten.

1 packet instant dry yeast
3 c. water (approximate), divided
2 1/2 lbs. flour
3 eggs, divided

1 TBSP margarine
1/4 c. sugar, divided
1 TBSP salt

In a large bowl, dissolve yeast in 1/2 c. warm water with a dash of sugar. Let stand 5–10 minutes until yeast bubbles. Sift flour into bowl and add 2 eggs, margarine, remaining sugar, salt, and water, reserving some of the water if needed. Stir to form a ball. Knead dough until smooth and elastic, about 12–15 minutes by hand. Place dough in a greased bowl, cover with a clean towel, and let rise until doubled in bulk, about one hour. Punch down and let rise another 30 minutes. Divide into two or three equal parts. For a round loaf, form into one large loaf shape and twist once to form a round shape. For a braided loaf, separate each ball in thirds and roll into a long shape. Braid loosely. Place on baking pan and let rise another 30 minutes before baking. Brush an egg over the loaves.

Set pan in a cool oven. Turn oven to 425 for the first 30 minutes and then bake for an additional 30–40 minutes at 350 degrees.

By custom there are two challahs on the Shabbat table, and after they are blessed they are eaten with salt. The salt symbolizes the concept of the brokenness of the world and the Jewish responsibility to fix it. Although the bread is called challah, the challah itself is actually a small piece of the bread that is taken after it has been formed into a loaf and is either burned in the oven or thrown in the trash can. In the times of the Temple, challah was taken from all foods and given to the high priests as a type of thanks or payment. Today people take this small portion only from challah, and possibly other cake and bread doughs. For many it has come to represent the connection between the mundane act of food preparation to God. It is a commandment for women to make challah every week.

Many American Jews wishing to be involved both in Jewish and American customs and culture stop their Shabbat observance here. They pause to recognize Shabbat, say the appropriate blessings, and may go out to dinner, a movie, or do some schoolwork. Many rabbis encourage American Jews to do whatever they can to mark Shabbat as an important part of the week, and it is primarily for this reason that Shabbat observance is so varied.

Before discussing traditional Shabbat and other holiday meals it is important to note that although there are many customary foods for Shabbat and other occasions, American Jews are often just as immersed in American culture as they are in Jewish culture. Jewish American cooks will often make ethnic foods such as French, Mexican, Middle Eastern, Asian, and Italian dishes for Shabbat dinner, although often adapted to be kosher or kosher-style. Additionally, American regional cuisine is just as influential on Jewish American cooks as it is on non-Jewish American cooks. Those who have a formal Shabbat dinner do not necessarily eat the traditional Shabbat foods; however, they do ensure that the Shabbat dinner is different from the rest of the week and is sufficiently special.

In an Ashkenazi home Shabbat dinner customarily begins with an appetizer such as traditional chicken soup with either *kreplach* or matzah balls. *Kreplach* are pasta dumplings filled with ground beef, which are either boiled or fried in chicken fat (schmaltz) or oil. Matzah balls are made from matzah meal (a flour-like powder made from matzah crackers) and eggs. This paste is then formed into balls and simmered. Each family has a different recipe for chicken soup; however, most involve some combination of carrots, onions, celery, turnips, dill, parsley, and a variety of chicken pieces, sometimes including the heart and gizzard. This deliciously fatty soup is thought by many to heal any ailment and to warm up each person at the table from the inside out.

Matzah Balls (*Knaidlach*)

2 eggs	1/4 c. club soda
2 TBSP oil	matzah meal as needed,
1 tsp salt	about 1 1/2 cups
1/4 tsp pepper	

Combine first five ingredients. Add matzah meal just enough to form a moldable consistency, like a meatball. Chill 30 minutes or up to 24 hours. Form into balls and drop into simmering water or chicken soup. Cook about 20 minutes and serve immediately or remove from liquid and serve later.

For a lighter texture separate eggs and fold in beaten egg whites to mixture.

The chicken soup is usually followed or preceded by gefilte fish, a Yiddish term meaning stuffed fish, or, in this case, fish stuffing. This is considered a delicacy in many circles and is a ground white fish, usually carp, that is formed into large quenelles and seasoned with onions, garlic, salt, and black pepper and then poached in water. It is served cold or at room temperature and is accompanied by a small green salad and a strong serving of fresh or jarred horseradish. There are a multitude of traditions surrounding gefilte fish. Although there are many brands that are now sold in jars, and many delis make their own for people to buy, there are still people who buy whole fish (usually carp) and clean, grind, and cook it themselves. Older generations often recount tales of keeping the carp in the bathtub until it is ready to be cooked.

"Doctored" Gefilte Fish

Like many Americans, Jewish Americans are busy and often use packaged and convenience foods. For holidays, though, such foods might be "doctored" or changed to more closely resemble the homemade version.

2 TBSP vegetable oil	1/4 tsp ground black pepper
1/2 c. onion, diced	1 dash paprika
1/2 c. celery, diced	1 carrot, sliced
1 27-ounce jar gefilte fish	

In a large pot, heat oil. Sauté onion and celery until limp. Add liquid from jar of fish, black pepper, and paprika and mix well. Add fish and carrots and cook until carrots are just tender. Can also be roasted in oven. Chill fish and gravy until ready to serve.

Serve gefilte fish on a lettuce leaf garnished with a sliced carrot. Serve with prepared horseradish as an accompaniment.

Whether in cutlets or on the bone, baked, fried, broiled, or grilled, chicken is the centerpiece of Shabbat dinner. It is often a challenge for cooks to create a chicken dish that will stand up to the warming process without drying out or overcooking. A classic Sabbath meal is chicken in the pot. A chicken is simmered with vegetables and the result is a two-course meal. First the soup, followed by the chicken. Many contemporary Jewish American recipes for chicken involve onion soup mix to give the chicken a quick and distinctive flavor. Cooks will often concoct a multitude of sauces in order to mask the dryness of the chicken that often comes from the advanced cooking and rewarming. Common ingredients found in Shabbat chicken are orange juice, honey, soy sauce, onions, garlic, ketchup, bread crumbs, and barbeque sauce.

The chicken is accompanied by a number of different side dishes. Jerusalem kugel, or kugel *yerushalmi,* is a sweet and spicy noodle pudding made with spaghetti, black pepper, sugar, and nondairy margarine. Also, some sort of plain boiled vegetable, such as string beans or broccoli, is usually served. In place of kugel *yerushalmi* can be any number of starchy side dishes: potato kugel, roasted or boiled potatoes, wild rice, couscous, or pasta.

Dessert at an Ashkenazi table is always an event. Hot fruit compote with a mix of canned, fresh, and dried fruit is served alongside tea and coffee to provide a tart sweetness to the end of the meal. Additionally, Ashkenazi Jews eat *schnecken* and *babka. Schnecken,* also known as *rugelach,* are small rolled pastry dough cookies stuffed with preserves, dried fruit, nuts, chocolate, or cinnamon. They are rolled in melted margarine and are baked until they are crispy. *Babka* is a sweet spongy yeast-based coffee cake that is swirled with chocolate or cinnamon and raisins, is baked in a loaf, and is often glazed or flavored with rum. Just like all other traditional Jewish meals, the blessing after the meal is recited at the end of dessert; however, there are special selections to add for Shabbat.

Sephardi Shabbat dinners also begin with the consumption of challah and wine. After that, the challah is enjoyed with a multitude of different cold salads. Depending on the region from which the family comes, the table may be filled with hummus (a ground chickpea and sesame paste dip), grilled eggplant salad, Israeli chopped salad (fresh tomatoes, cucumber, onion, and dill), chopped liver, minted couscous salad, *baba ganoush* (roasted eggplant blended with mayonnaise), or Turkish salad (stewed tomatoes and garlic with herbs).

After the salads many families serve a Sephardi version of gefilte fish. It may be made with any white fish and is cooked with tomatoes, onions, and spices. Another appetizer could be any kind of soup that is particular to the family's origin; Greek Jews may serve *avolgomeno,* Italian Jews may make lentil or tomato and bread soup, Spanish Jews are likely to eat leek soup, and Egyptian or Syrian Jews often eat a red lentil soup. Common main courses at a Sephardi Shabbat dinner table vary. One dish frequently served at Shabbat dinners is a brisket (pot roast) slowly cooked with string beans, tomatoes, garlic, and other seasonings.

Breakfast is not included as one of the three meals of Shabbat; therefore, those who wish to eat something in the morning cannot eat any bread or anything that would qualify as a substantial meal. Breakfast is often eaten before leaving for synagogue and is a light meal composed of fruit, cakes, coffee, tea, or cereal. Many observant Jews skip breakfast altogether on Shabbat in order to make sure they have only three meals.

American Jews are so heavily involved with food on Shabbat that there is even plentiful food during synagogue. It is an American custom to have "Kiddush Clubs," or groups of men who leave the service during the reading of the prophets to enjoy some schnapps, herring, cheese, crackers, and cakes. Although heavy drinking has become a problem in some communities during these meetings, people continue to meet, eat, and drink.

After services at both Sephardi and Ashkenazi synagogues there is a kiddush, or small snack. The original purpose of this practice was to make sure that all who were present were able to hear the blessing over the wine for Shabbat afternoon. Now, however, kiddush at American synagogues has become an institution unto itself. While some synagogues still have just a small selection of cakes, challah, and drinks, it is now more common to have an elaborate display of fruit, brownies, cookies, cakes, herring, whitefish, bagels and cream cheese, chocolates, and an impressive amount of liquor. When there is an event at the synagogue, such as a bar or bat mitzvah, a baby naming, or some other happy occasion, the regular kiddush is supplemented with varieties of smoked and pickled fish, blintzes (crepes with fruit or cheese filling), salads, pasta dishes, or kugels.

Shabbat lunch is the second major meal of Shabbat. It presents even more challenges than Shabbat dinner because of the issue of cooking and reheating. Challah and wine are eaten and blessed at this meal, and it is a leisurely time to eat, drink, talk, and enjoy visitors and company. It is a custom in both Ashkenazi and Sephardi American communities to make slow-cooked dishes for this meal that require little attention once Shabbat begins. Historically these dishes would have been placed in a cooling community brick oven, after the baking of the challah, and consumed, still warm, the next day. These days, a crock pot or slow cooker is an essential tool in the traditional Jewish American home in order to make stews, soups, and other hearty dishes.

Cholent is a food that is central to both Sephardi and Ashkenazi traditional lunch meals. It is a meat (or possibly vegetarian) stew comprised of beans, stew beef, and often tomatoes. The cook puts all of the ingredients into the slow cooker or pot hours before Shabbat and allows the stew to cook, leaving it warming in its cooking vessel until it is ready to be served.

Sephardi *cholents* usually have chickpeas and barley in them, in addition to dried fruit, tomatoes, and cinnamon. It is also a popular practice to cook a few eggs in with the *cholent* so that the permeable eggshell allows for the fragrance of the stew to permeate into the egg itself. Ashkenazi *cholents* are more likely to include kidney beans, lima beans, barley, tomato, paprika, onion, and garlic. The result is a hearty stick-to-your ribs dish.

Cholent

1 c. brown pinto beans, washed and soaked overnight	2 beef marrow bones
1 c. white beans, washed and soaked overnight	1 lb. tough cut of beef like brisket, round, or shin
1 onion, coarsely chopped	water to cover
4 cloves garlic, smashed	Salt, pepper, and paprika to taste

Place all ingredients together in a pot. Bring to boil, cover and cook on low flame until beans are tender, about three hours. Check occasionally for sticking and add water as needed.

Another slow-cooked dish often made for Shabbat lunch is kishka. This is stuffed derma or cow intestine (although there are also methods for making it vegetarian). It is sewn and may be cooked either in the *cholent* or roasted separately. It is a comfort food favorite for many and is generally served only on Shabbat. Eastern European Jews stuff their kishka with bread crumbs, egg, onion, spices, and chicken fat, while Sephardi Jews use nuts, meat, vegetables, and dried fruit.

Finally, many Yemenite Jewish families make *kubbanah*, a Shabbat overnight bread. It is a yeast bread that often includes caraway seeds and is cooked in a pot in the embers of a fire overnight in a special *kubbanah* pot or in a normal casserole dish. Many people have the custom of placing raw eggs on top of the bread and baking them along with it.

The third meal of Shabbat, also known as *seudah shlisheet* or *shala shudis*, is a time in which to lengthen the peaceful mood of Shabbat for as long as possible. There is often a mournful tone to the meal, as the forthcoming departure of Shabbat is distressing. This is often a light meal, as people have eaten so much during the day and often have plans to go out after Shabbat. Sephardi families may eat small amounts of pita bread with a variety of salads, and Ashkenazi Jews are likely to eat tuna fish, egg salad, whitefish salad, bagels, and so on. It is rarely a meat meal.

Shabbat is ended with a service called havdala. It is a time in which to bring in the coming week with sweetness and joy and to bid farewell to Shabbat. Among other things, part of the havdala service is to inhale a pleasing scent such as cinnamon, cloves, or citrus. It is at this point that the 25-hour eating extravaganza comes to an end and people go back to their weekly routines.

ROSH HASHANA

Rosh Hashana, or Head of the Year, is the Jewish New Year (although it is actually the seventh month in the 12 or 13 month calendar). It is a holiday that commemorates the birthday of the world and is one in which Jews become introspective about who they are, who they have been, and who they will be in the future. The liturgy of Rosh Hashana is largely based on the themes of repentance and God's sovereignty and was instituted in its original form in Leviticus 23:24–25, in which it says, "Speak to the children of Israel, saying: In the seventh month, in the first day of the month, shall be a solemn rest for you, a memorial proclaimed with the blast of horns, a holy convocation. You shall do no manner of servile work; and you shall bring an offering made by fire unto the Lord." This is a holiday that includes many Shabbat-type observances, so no work is permitted and much of the day is spent in synagogue. The holiday marks the beginning of a 10-day period of reflection, communion with God, and atonement, which concludes with the observance of Yom Kippur. Rosh Hashanah is one of the most important holidays of the year for Jews, and many mark it with festive holiday meals and with attending synagogue.

During Rosh Hashanah, it is traditional to eat apples dipped in honey to symbolize the hope for a "sweet" new year. The apple is dipped in honey, the blessing for eating tree fruits is recited, the apple is tasted, and then the apples and honey prayer is recited. The primary reason most rabbis give for eating apples on Rosh Hashanah is that apples were the most readily available fruit in the areas where most Jews of antiquity lived. Honey has a particular significance to Jews because Israel is often referred to in the Torah as "the land of milk and honey."

In addition to apples and honey, Sephardi and Ashkenazi Jews alike bake a special round challah on Rosh Hashana, usually with extra honey in it. The roundness of the challah symbolizes continuity and the hope for a well-rounded year. Many Moroccan Jews make a special round cake-like challah on Rosh Hashana that is fragranced with anise. Often people will dip their challah in honey instead of salt to further the sweetness of the moment. Many families will continue to eat round challah instead of the long loaf-style challah throughout the rest of the autumnal holidays as a reminder of the important philosophical and liturgical ideas of Rosh Hashana.

The other major food of Rosh Hashana is the pomegranate. There are a variety of reasons that the pomegranate is featured during this holiday. First, it is thought of as a biblical fruit. The rabbis suggest that there are 613 seeds in a pomegranate, which is the exact number of commandments in the Torah.

When eating a pomegranate on Rosh Hashana there is a special blessing to recite: "May it be Your will that our merits be numerous as (the seeds of) the pomegranate." By eating the pomegranate, Jews figuratively show their desire and hope to fulfill all 613 commandments. Different families have different customs concerning the use of the pomegranate in the meal. Often, pomegranate seeds are placed on the table to nibble during the meal. Other people cook with the pomegranate and make things like pomegranate glazed chicken, roasted vegetables with pomegranate seeds, or salad with a pomegranate dressing.

There is a custom among Sephardi Jews to have a short service, or seder, before the Rosh Hashana dinner, which includes a variety of foods that symbolize different important aspects of the holiday. Each food has its own verse that accompanies it, and each food is eaten individually. Most of the foods are eaten because the Hebrew name for them sounds like a word that is tied into the themes of Rosh Hashana. First, dates are eaten because the Hebrew word for date, *tamar*, is from the same root as the word to cease, *yitamoo* (the root is *tam*). The date is eaten and a prayer is said to ask God to stop the suffering of the Jewish people at the hand of their foes. Next, the biblical pomegranate is eaten, followed by the apples and honey. Following this typical beginning to the service come some other interesting additions to the Rosh Hashana meal. A cooked squash or other gourd is placed on the table and participants say, "May it be the will of our Heavenly Father that any bad decree be torn up and that our merits be read before You," since the Hebrew word for squash, *k'ra'a*, sounds like the word for tear, *yikaru*. After this, the participants eat cooked black-eyed peas. The symbolism of this food is that the word in Hebrew for black-eyed peas, *rubiya*, is similar to the word for many, *rov*; by eating the peas, those at the table are asking God for their good merits to increase. Interestingly, black-eyed peas are also a common New Years food for African Americans. Next are leeks, followed by beets. Leeks are eaten because the word for leek, *karti*, is similar to the word for cut down, *karat*, and beets are eaten because the word for beet, *silka*, sounds like the word for removed, *salak*. The seder participants ask that their enemies be cut down and removed. Finally, a fish head is split among those present to ask God for the blessing of posterity, and a ram's head is eaten to simply symbolize the head of the New Year.

Most Ashkenazi Rosh Hashana dinners bypass this custom and start off with a traditional chicken soup with either kreplach or matzah balls. Cooks hoping to modernize the Rosh Hashana meal may make any variation of this soup, including Chinese-style dumplings, matzah balls filled with anything from saffron to spinach, and soup with butternut squash or asparagus.

There are a variety of Sephardi versions of chicken soup that are also served as a first course. Yemenite Jews are likely to use turnips, zucchini, and tomato in their chicken soup and to flavor it with a variety of Yemenite spices, while Jews of a Mediterranean origin may add saffron or leeks to their broth. Moroccans often add chickpeas and beef bones to their soup, and Israelis fill theirs with fragrant herbs. Instead of soup, many Sephardi Jews serve spice-infused stuffed dried fruit. Figs or prunes are stuffed with meat, onions, and nuts, and cooked in liquid with oil, water, red wine, and seasonings.

The main course of a Rosh Hashana dinner varies by tradition and can include any number of time-honored or ethnic and regional dishes. A typical Ashkenazi dinner usually has a brisket, or pot roast, as its main feature. Though methods and ingredients differ, the brisket is always slow-cooked (either in the oven or stovetop) and frequently includes onions and perhaps something to add some sweetness, such as honey or dried fruit. Some cooks make their briskets with a tomato base with canned tomatoes or tomato paste. Different liquids are used to infuse the brisket with flavor. Some use red wine or vinegar, while others use stock, tomato sauce, or onion soup mix. Another popular main item for Rosh Hashana is roast duck, the sweet and fat flesh connotative of a rich and sweet new year.

A popular Ashkenazi side dish on Rosh Hashana is tzimmes, or sweetened carrots. The carrots are cooked until they are extremely tender, and some combinations of raisins, sugar, honey, and cinnamon are added to create a sweet and delicious carrot stew. Some cooks make a variation on tzimmes with sweet potatoes or different squashes.

The main courses and side dishes at a Sephardi Rosh Hashana dinner differ greatly according to the origin of the family. In truth, there are not many dishes that are made specifically for Rosh Hashana. Rather, like the Ashkenazi serving roast duck or brisket, Sephardi Jews adapt recipes of their regions for the Rosh Hashana table. For example, those with Moroccan roots may make a chicken *tagine* with couscous, while those from Greece may make an adaptation of moussaka. It is also customary for Sephardi Jews to eat string beans on Rosh Hashana.

For both Sephardi and Ashkenazi Jews, dessert is a time to again showcase the ever-present apples and honey of Rosh Hashana. Honey cake and apple cake are the two reigning desserts on Ashkenazi tables. Honey cake is a simple cake with large quantities of honey. The cake becomes moister and its flavors deepen a day or two after it is baked. Jewish apple cake is some form of a pound cake recipe that is laced with slices of apples and cinnamon and usually has a sticky apple topping. Many people also make *tayglach,* which are dough balls that are stuffed with raisins or nuts, seasoned with lemon or ginger, and cooked in honey syrup to a rich mahogany color. Moroccan and other North African Jews make *cigares,* which are dainty finger pastries oozing with honey syrup.

Lunch after synagogue on Rosh Hashana, although not as elaborate as the dinners, is always a culinary event. Though some American Jewish families opt to simply serve leftovers, many others make entirely separate meals. There are no foods that are particular to Rosh Hashana lunch other than those previously mentioned for Shabbat; it is simply relevant to note that this meal is an important one.

YOM KIPPUR

Yom Kippur is a holiday that ironically and accurately portrays the typical Jewish relationship with food. Yom Kippur is a fast day and is the most important and introspective holiday of the Jewish calendar, marked by the absence of food. However, there is still an assortment of foods that are heavily associated with Yom Kippur and are enjoyed before and after the fast. Food is such an integral part of Jewish culture in America that even the most important fast day of the year has large sections devoted to it in every Jewish American holiday cookbook.

The 10-day period between Rosh Hashana and Yom Kippur is a time for self-examination and atonement. These 10 days of repentance offer the opportunity for people to ask for forgiveness from each other and God and culminate in the holiest day of the year, Yom Kippur. On Yom Kippur, God's judgment of each human being is entered in "The Book of Life" and is sealed. This day is essentially the last chance to change the judgment and to demonstrate repentance through making amends. Yom Kippur is thought of as the holiest day of the year, and traditional Jews refrain not only from eating and drinking, but also from bathing, brushing teeth, applying makeup, and wearing leather, because all of these things are traditional markers of luxury. Many secular Jews fast and attend synagogue on Yom Kippur, where the number of worshippers attending is often double or triple the normal attendance.

The pre-fast meal is usually an early one, because people want to get to synagogue to get good seats and to be there for the beginning of the evening service promptly at sundown. It is a custom in Ashkenazi communities to eat meat kreplach right before fasting. The meat symbolizes God's inflexible justice and the soft dough symbolizes God's compassion and ability to forgive. The kreplach are either boiled in water or fried in chicken fat. Aside from kreplach, there are no true traditional foods to eat before Yom Kippur. Whoever is doing the cooking usually tries to avoid overly spicy food, caffeine, and salt with the hopes of making the fast easier for those eating the meal. A plain boiled chicken with boiled potatoes is sometimes served; however, most American Jews desire more of a substantial meal than that and make different types of chicken and starch dishes to help fasters deal with the 25 hours without food. Those Sephardi Jews willing to put forth the effort traditionally make almond milk before the fast to strengthen the body and ready the mind for prayer. The almonds are ground finely and are then wrapped in cheese cloth and immersed in water. Later they are boiled and sweetened.

After spending a full 25 hours without any food or water, people certainly begin to get hungry. The meal to break the fast is almost always dairy and is one in which it is just as common to dine with family as it is with friends. In Ashkenazi communities the meal is an elaborate spread, often a buffet, with only an entrée and dessert course. Bagels, multiple varieties of smoked salmon, cream cheese, cheese, and vegetables all hold a primary place on the Ashkenazi table.

In addition to all of these foods there is pickled herring or herring in sour cream, which is often enjoyed on its own or with pieces of challah. While many American Jews now buy their pickled herring or herring in sour cream at delis or kosher supermarkets, there are still some people who go to the efforts of making their own. The cleansed herring is soaked in a mixture of vinegar, lemon, sugar, and seasonings. After sitting in a cool place for a few days, sour cream and other ingredients may be added.

Additionally, many people make a dairy kugel, which is a sweet and creamy noodle pudding. Egg noodles are combined with any combination of cream cheese, cottage cheese, cream, milk, and sour cream and enhanced with cinnamon, sugar, fruit, and occasionally a crispy topping of nuts or buttered cornflakes. The kugel is baked in a casserole dish and served warm. Like much Jewish food, it improves a day or two later.

Cakes, pastries, and fresh fruit are common desserts.

Sephardi Jews vary in their customs for the meal that breaks the fast. To break the fast Sephardi Jews may munch on little round biscuits like mini-bagels with sesame seeds and spices to soothe the stomach, along with a cup of sweetened tea. Moroccan and other North African Jews commonly make *harira,* a soup made of chickpeas (or other beans) and barley, tomato, onion, and celery. However, Sephardi Jews frequently eat a light dairy meal at sundown and wait until later in the evening to consume a heavier meat meal. This meal may consist of any food that is typical of the region and is relatively quick and easy to prepare.

SUKKOT, SHMINI ATZERET, AND SIMHAT TORAH

Sukkot, also known as the Feast of Tabernacles, is one of the three pilgrimage holidays in the Jewish calendar. It commemorates the 40-year period during which the Israelites were wandering in the desert, living in temporary shelters. The word *sukkot* literally means booths and refers to the temporary dwelling in which Jews are supposed to live and eat during the holiday. Although most American Jews do not sleep in the sukkot, those who build them (there are many specifications for how to build a sukkah) eat most of their meals there.

Sukkot lasts for seven days. The two days following the festival, Shemini Atzeret and Simhat Torah, are separate holidays but are related to Sukkot

Festive Sukkot meal. Courtesy of Rabbi
Moshe and Meira Saks.

and are commonly thought of as part of Sukkot. One of the commandments
during Sukkot is to rejoice and be happy, which is often understood as an ex-
cuse to consume large quantities of alcohol, especially during Simhat Torah.

In America Sukkot is bookended with two festive days at the beginning
and two at the end. Like the holiday of Passover, Sukkot includes *hag* days
and *hol ha moed* days. The *hag* days bookend the week of Sukkot; there are
two at the beginning and two at the end. *Hag* is marked with Shabbat-type
observances, such as the abstention from work and cooking and attendance
at synagogue. The days in the middle, *hol ha moed*, are still festive but do not
require any observance other than eating and sleeping in the sukkah.

One observance during Sukkot involves what is known as the Four Species
(*arba minim* in Hebrew) or the *lulav* and *etrog*. Jews are commanded to take
these four plants and use them to "rejoice before the Lord." The four species
in question are an *etrog* (a citrus fruit similar to a lemon native to Israel; in
English it is called a citron), a palm branch (in Hebrew, *lulav*), two willow
branches (*aravot*) and three myrtle branches (*hadassim*). After Sukkot is over
many families turn their *etrog* into a jam or stud it with cloves to be used at
the end of Shabbat for the coming year with the hope of bringing the sweet
smell into the week ahead.

Simchat Torah means "Rejoicing in the Torah." This holiday marks the
completion of the annual cycle of weekly Torah readings. Each week in

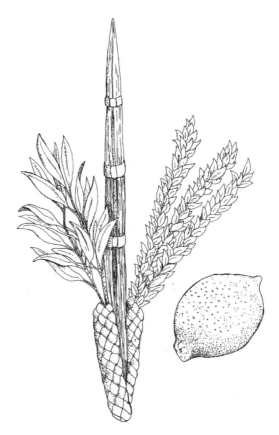

Lulav and *etrog*: the four species. © J. Susan Cole Stone.

synagogue Jews publicly read a few chapters from the Torah, starting with Genesis 1 and working their way around to Deuteronomy 34. On Simchat Torah, they read the last Torah portion and then proceed immediately to the first chapter of Genesis, reminding them that the Torah is a circle that never ends. This completion of the readings is a time of great celebration. There are processions around the synagogue carrying Torah scrolls and plenty of high-spirited singing and dancing with the Torahs.

The meals that take place during the *hag* days of sukkot are festive ones that include many typical Jewish foods. However, there are two major culinary traditions on Sukkot. One is to serve any dish incorporating the harvest of one's own region. The other widespread tradition on Sukkot among Ashkenazi and Sephardi Jews alike is to serve stuffed dishes to symbolize the abundance that Sukkot celebrates. One common practice among Ashkenazi Jews is to serve sweet and sour stuffed cabbage (*praches*) as an appetizer on this holiday. Though time-consuming to assemble, this hearty beef dish is an appetizer worthy of a cold night in the sukkah. A head of green cabbage, which is a harvest vegetable of the Eastern European Ashkenazi Jews, is boiled whole and then carefully disassembled, leaf by leaf. Each piece is individually stuffed with a mixture of ground beef and any combination of onions, rice, garlic, eggs, salt, and pepper. A tomato-based sweet and sour sauce is then made with ketchup, brown sugar, vinegar, raisins, citrus juice, cinnamon, onion, tomato sauce, and water, or some variation thereof. The sauce is then layered in a stockpot with the stuffed cabbage leaves and left to cook slowly on the stovetop for at least an hour and a half until the flavors have blended together.

Stuffed Cabbage (Sephardi Style)

8 savoy or green cabbage leaves for stuffing

Filling

1 onion, chopped   1 c. rice
1/2 tsp cumin   2 TBSP chopped parsley
1/4 tsp turmeric   salt and ground pepper to
1/2 lb. ground lamb   taste

Sauce

3 TBSP olive oil   1/2 tsp cumin
1 medium onion, minced   1/4 tsp turmeric
2 garlic cloves, minced   2 3/4 c. chicken broth
1 TBSP tomato paste

Prepare the cabbage leaves for stuffing by removing the tough stem and blanching in boiling water until soft.

Filling: Mix the filling ingredients together. Place a large spoonful (meatball size) of the meat on each leaf. Roll like an egg roll or burrito. Place in a greased pot.

Sauce: Sauté the onion in the oil until soft. Add the garlic, tomato paste, and spices and cook for one minute. Add broth and bring to a boil, whisking in spices and tomato paste.

Cover the cabbage rolls with sauce and simmer, covered, about one hour.

Instead of cabbage, Sephardi Jews stuff things like peppers and zucchini on Sukkot, since those are some of the harvest vegetables of the Sephardi regions. The stuffed vegetables are made with either ground meat or a mix of cheese and breadcrumbs and are always heavily seasoned with the spices and herbs of each particular region. Moroccan Jews also serve couscous at this time to again symbolize abundance. Additionally, Syrian Jews make *kahk,* sesame-sprinkled rounds of crumbly pastry; the sesame seeds again signify abundance.

Simhat Torah does not have any true separate food traditions from the rest of Sukkot. However, one new tradition is for particularly involved and adept cooks to create foods such as challahs, cakes, casseroles, cookies, and other dishes in the shape of a Torah scroll.

HANUKKAH

Hanukkah, also known as the Festival of Lights, is extremely different from the first three holidays of the Jewish calendar. First, Hanukkah is not a holiday of biblical origin; rather, it is a Talmudic holiday, which marks the miraculous victory of the Jews, led by the Maccabees, against Greek persecution and religious oppression. Hanukkah is celebrated by giving gelt, or small amounts of money. Because Hanukkah is usually around Christmas-time in America, American Jews changed the tradition of giving gelt to a tradition of gift-giving (although there are some traditional Jews who still only give gelt). Hanukkah is not marked by any observance of not working or extra prayers. It is a time to be with family and to celebrate the resilience of the Jewish people.

In addition to the Maccabees being victorious in war, another miracle occurred on Hanukkah: when they came to rededicate the Temple, they found only one flask of oil with which to light the menorah (the lamp), enough for a few hours of light. This small flask lasted for eight days. In order to commemorate this miracle, Jews light a menorah, or eight-pronged candelabra, for the eight days of Hanukkah. It is for this reason that all traditional Hanukkah recipes from all regions include large amounts of oil and usually involve deep frying.

The most universal Ashkenazi Hanukkah dish is surely potato latkes. Enjoyed with applesauce, sour cream, or caviar, these hot cakes go well with breakfast, lunch, or dinner and can be featured as either an appetizer or a main course. Traditional potato latkes combine shredded potatoes and onions, egg, salt, and pepper into a flat patty. The patty is then fried in vegetable oil on both sides to produce a delightfully crispy treat. Variations on potato latkes differ by region, and some cooks may include sweet potatoes, shredded apples, or zucchini in the latkes. Some people do not make potato latkes because they are too labor-intensive and instead opt to make a potato kugel.

Potato Latkes

6 potatoes, grated	1 tsp salt
1 small onion, grated	1/4 tsp pepper
3 eggs	oil for frying
1/4 c. flour or matzah meal	

Mix all ingredients in a large bowl. In a large frying pan, heat oil. Gently drop spoonfuls of potato mixture into hot oil and fry on both sides until brown.

Another popular Ashkenazi snack to enjoy year-round, but especially on Hanukkah, is *gribenes*. This is a type of chicken chip that is made by rendering the fat of chicken skin strips and then frying it in its own fat with onions. *Gribenes* is lightly salted and eaten throughout the day. The leftover chicken fat, or schmaltz, is reserved for future cooking.

Sephardi Jews, especially those in Israel, feast on *sufganiyot* on Hanukkah. These moist and cakey jelly doughnuts are fried and covered in powdered sugar for a dessert that again commemorates the miracle of Hanukkah with the use of oil. Many American Ashkenazi Jews also indulge in *sufaniyot* over Hanukkah because of their mouth-watering texture and sweet insides. Jewish bakeries make huge quantities of *sufganiyot* for Hanukkah and people buy them for parties, gift exchanges, Hebrew school, and religious day school. Additionally, many Spanish Jews eat *bimuelos* (or *buneolos*) on Hanukkah. They are also a fried yeast dough, covered in honey while they are still hot.

One of the Hanukkah legends involves Judith, who also met the Syrians and defeated them. It is said that she defeated the general by intoxicating him with succulent cheese and ample wine, which is why many Sephardi Jews serve different types of cheese pancakes, or *sambusak*. Italian Jews make ricotta pancakes, while Greek Jews make theirs with feta cheese.

Jelly Doughnuts for Hanukkah

1 packet active dry yeast	1 pinch salt
1/2 c. warm water	oil for frying
2 c. flour	confectioners sugar for dust-
1 egg	ing
1 TBSP sugar	jelly for filling

In medium bowl combine yeast and warm water. Add remaining ingredients and knead until a smooth dough is formed. Let rise one hour, punch down and let rise another 30 minutes. Roll on a clean surface to about 1/2–1/4 inch thickness. Cut into 1 1/2 inch squares or rounds. Fry in hot oil until doughnuts puff and brown on both sides. Drain onto paper towels and let cool. Meanwhile fill a pastry bag with jelly. When cool enough to handle, fill doughnuts with jelly from pastry bag. Dust with powdered sugar.

TU BISHVAT

Though it is in winter, the fifteenth day of the Hebrew month of *Shvat* is the "New Year" of the trees, a time to stop and reflect on the many blessings that the land gives. It not a Torah holiday and has no commandments associated with it. It is, however, discussed at length in the Talmud. Tu Bishvat was origi-nally a day when the fruits that grew from that day on were counted for the following year regarding tithes (taxes Jews paid with agriculture). During the Middle Ages or possibly a little before that, this day started to be celebrated with a minor ceremony of eating fruits, since the Mishnah called it Rosh Ha-shanah (New Year), and that was later understood as being a time appropriate for celebration. It was from this that a short Tu Bishvat seder was developed. In America, especially in Hebrew schools and religious schools, Tu Bishvat is celebrating by planting trees and taking part in the small seder, or service.

During the seder it is customary to eat different types of fruit on this holi-day and to recite the appropriate blessings. Many people also eat all kinds of dried fruit as well, such as raisins and nuts. Traditionally, these types of fruit and grains are: wheat, barley, grapes, figs, pomegranates, olives, and dates (there are the seven species associated with the land of Israel in the Torah). Also, fruits and nuts with hard, inedible exteriors and soft edible insides, such as oranges, bananas, walnuts, and pistachios are eaten along with fruits and nuts with soft exteriors, but with a hard pit inside, such as dates, apricots, olives, and per-simmons. Finally, there are fruits that are eaten whole, such as figs and berries.

Meals on Tu Bishvat use a mixture of these fruits and nuts to continue the theme of the holiday; however, there are few dishes particular to Tu Bishvat itself.

PURIM

Like Hanukkah and Tu Bishvat, Purim is also a holiday that is not commanded by the Torah but is one that is discussed in the Talmud. Also like Hanukkah, Purim is a holiday that celebrates a historic Jewish victory over enemies. The story of Purim comes from the section of the Hebrew Bible called the Writings, in the book of Esther, which is the third section of the *Tanach*, or Jewish bible. The reason for celebrating Purim comes from the verses, "And they gained relief on the fourteenth, making it a day of feasting and gladness" (Esther 9:17) and, "[Mordecai instructed them] to observe them as days of feasting and gladness, and sending delicacies to one another, and gifts to the poor" (Esther 9:22).

The book of Esther tells how Esther, the niece of Mordechai, came to be the king of Persia's wife. He had an evil advisor named Haman who hated the Jews and plotted to kill them. When Esther learned of this scheme she told her uncle, who in turn told her to tell the king. When the king heard of this and found out that Esther, too, was Jewish, he saved the Jews and had Haman executed.

The main commandment of Purim is to hear the recitation of the book of Esther. However, it is also a commandment on this day to eat, drink, and be merry. According to the Talmud a person is supposed to drink until he cannot tell the difference between the cursed Haman and the blessed Mordechai. Purim is a carnival-like holiday in which adults and children dress up in costumes of the characters of the story of Purim or of any other funny thing or persona. It is a holiday of rowdiness, performances, jokes, fun, and always a great deal of food.

In addition, it is customary to send out gifts of food or drink, and to make gifts to charity. The sending of gifts of food and drink is referred to as *shalach manot* (literally, sending out portions) and comes from the section of the book of Esther in which Mordechai tells the people to send out food to each other. Synagogues and other Jewish organizations often assemble these for all of their members or sell them. The *shalach manot* include an assortment of cookies, candy, bread, chocolate, and drinks among other things. There are many people who assemble their own packages and distribute them to family and friends.

Depending on whether one is Ashkenazi or Sephardi, the food most associated with Purim is either hamantaschen or *oznei haman*, which are the same food with different names. Hamantaschen are a pastry that originated in Germany. They are triangular and are traditionally filled with a sticky poppy seed filling; however, many American Jews fill theirs with a cherry pie filling, chocolate chips, fruit preserves, marshmallow, or cream cheese. There are a number of different reasons given for the consumption of hamantaschen on Purim. Ashkenazi Jews say that Haman wore a triangular hat, and so we eat triangular cookies, while Sephardi Jews say that his ears were triangular. Others simply explain it by reasoning that *taschen* is the name for a pocket-like cookie in German, and *mun* is the word for poppy seed. When put together the sounds make *muntaschen*, which is similar to the name of Haman. It was perhaps in this way that *muntaschen* became a convenient cookie for Purim. It should also be noted that some German Jews make gingerbread men in the likeness of Haman and then eat them.

Hamantashen

4 eggs	2 tsp baking powder
1 c. sugar	jelly or canned poppy seed
1/2 c. oil	filling for filling
juice and rind of one lemon	1 egg for brushing
4 c. flour	

Preheat oven to 350 degrees. In a large bowl mix liquid ingredients. Sift dry ingredients into liquid ingredients and mix to form a ball. Chill about 20–30 minutes. On a floured surface, roll dough to 1/4–1/8 inch thickness. With a glass or round cutter, cut into 3-inch rounds. Place a spoonful of jelly or poppy seed filling in the center of each round. Form the triangle shape by pinching three corners together. Brush with beaten egg and bake about 15 minutes.

It is traditional to have a Purim *seudah* (feast) on Purim day. At this meal, some serve an especially long, braided challah (in memory of the rope used to hang Haman), soup with kreplach (triangular shaped in memory of Haman's hat), and turkey, in memory of King Ahasuerus's reign from Persia, which is *hodu* in Hebrew and is also translated as turkey. Others have a vegetarian meal, because Esther ate as a vegetarian in order to keep kosher in the king's palace. A side dish at the meal is frequently kasha *varnishkas*, which is a dish composed of buckwheat and bowtie-shaped pasta. The buckwheat (kasha) is toasted to develop the earthy, nutty flavor and is then combined with chicken fat, stock, onions, and eggs. Of course, for dessert there is hamantashen.

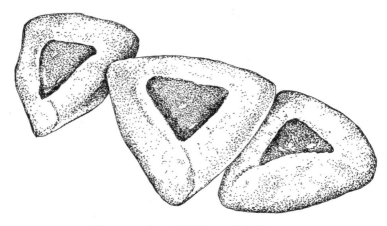

Hamantaschen. © J. Susan Cole Stone.

PASSOVER

Passover, in Hebrew Pesach, is the most food-obsessed holiday on the Jewish calendar. The observance of Passover stems from the Torah and from discussion of relevant passages in the Talmud. The reason for the holiday is to commemorate the departure of the Jews from Egypt out of slavery and into freedom. There are multiple food traditions included in the observance of Passover, most of which are commanded in the Torah. The primary observances of Passover are related to the Exodus from Egypt after generations of slavery. This story is told in Exodus, chapters 1–15. Many of the Passover observances are instituted in chapters 12–15.

Passover is another pilgrimage festival and is eight days long in the Diaspora. Like Sukkot, the first two days and the last two days of Passover are celebrated as *hag,* while the middle days are celebrated as *hol ha moed.* Passover is always a spring holiday and usually falls around the same time as Easter. Passover is said to be the most widely observed holiday by American Jews.

Probably the most significant observance related to Passover involves the removal of *chametz* (leaven) from the home. This commemorates the fact that the Jews leaving Egypt were in a hurry and did not have time to let their bread rise. It is also a symbolic way of removing the "puffiness" (arrogance, pride) from the soul.

Chametz includes anything made from the five major grains (wheat, rye, barley, oats, and spelt) that has not been completely cooked within 18 minutes after coming into contact with water. Ashkenazi Jews also avoid rice, corn, peanuts, and legumes as if they were *chametz.* All of these items are potentially used to make bread; thus, use of them was prohibited to avoid any confusion. Such additional items are referred to as *kitniyot* and are eaten by Sephardi Jews.

The issue with *chametz* on Passover has a number of implications for meals and food on Passover. Observant Jews rid their house of any products containing *chametz* and thoroughly clean the entire home, with special concentration on the kitchen. Separate dishes, pots, pans, utensils, and glasses are used on Passover to prevent any contact with *chametz*. Countertops and other food preparation areas are covered, and the *chametz* is either literally or figuratively sold to a non-Jew temporarily for the length of Passover.

The abstention from *chametz* on Passover has created an enormous industry for food referred to as "kosher for Passover." Leading up to Passover, Jewish and non-Jewish markets begin to stock special products without any *chametz*. Companies like Manischewitz, Gefen, Osem, and others make, among other things kosher for Passover, jams, sauces, soups, frozen meals, ice cream, candy, chocolate, salad dressing, condiments, snack foods, cheeses, yogurts, sodas, juices, and cereals. Many people will also only buy kosher for Passover milk, eggs, and even sometimes produce. Going shopping for Passover is an event unto itself, because the holiday requires that everything, even spices, be kosher for Passover.

The primary grain-product eaten on Passover is matzah. This is the replica of the uncooked bread the Jews made right before they left Egypt. The making of matzah is an arduous task because it requires that no more than 18 minutes should pass between the time the water touches the flour and the matzah is finished baking. Matzah is made only with cold water and a special flour called *kemach shel matzah shamura* (flour watched from the moment of harvest to the moment of packing to make sure it has not come into contact with any moisture). It is kneaded and rolled extremely thin, poked with holes, and then baked on tiles in an oven for two to three minutes.

Matzah is the base for many foods on Passover. Recipes that call for Matzah often use it as a replacement for bread, pasta, rice, barley, or other grains. Matzah is often ground up and referred to as matzah meal and is then used as a replacement for flour or breadcrumbs. Matzah is also often eaten on its own, or accompanied by butter, jam, cream cheese, tuna fish, or herring.

Two other ingredients, potato starch and cake meal, are also essential to cooking and baking on Passover. Potato starch is a powder used in place of cornstarch and is used not only to thicken dishes, but also to add a bit of tenderness to baked goods. Cake meal is a finer granulation of matzah meal. This sandy fine powder is used in most cakes. It works best in combination with matzah meal and potato starch for the most optimal balance between body and tenderness in the finished product.

The first two nights of Passover are marked with special dinners called seders. Although food is an extremely important aspect of the seder, the key reason for the seder is to recount the tale of the Israelite Exodus from Egypt. Originally written as part of the Talmud, the seder (which means order) is a lengthy service that includes teachings, songs, storytelling, blessings, and other prayers. The sequence of the seder is specific and extensive and encourages the participation of all present. A seder plate accompanies the text of the seder and includes different symbolic foods that are integral parts of the seder.

The seder begins with the blessing over the first cup of wine. Throughout the seder there are four cups of wine, and each cup receives a separate blessing. Next there is a ceremonial washing of the hands accompanied by another blessing. After this the seder participants eat the first of many foods. A vegetable such as celery or parsley is dipped in salt water, blessed, and then eaten. The vegetable represents springtime, and the salt water represents the tears of the enslaved Israelites. After this the leader of the table takes the pile of matzah on the table and breaks the middle piece in half. This piece is called the *afikomen* and will appear later in the seder.

Following the division of the middle matzah is the lengthiest part of the seder, the telling of the story of the Exodus from Egypt with accompanying sections from the Talmud. After this section is finished (in traditional circles it can take two or three hours) the preparations for the meal begin. The seder participants wash their hands a second time and then recite the *motzi*, the blessing that is usually said over bread, but during Passover is said over matzah. Next, each person at the table takes a small bit of horseradish *(marror)*

Matzah. Courtesy of Rachel Saks.

Seder plate. Courtesy of Rachel Saks.

on its own, and then combines it with a piece of matzah. The horseradish, often referred to as bitter herbs, symbolizes the bitterness with which the Israelites experienced slavery. The bitter herbs and matzah are then combined with a sweet and nutty chopped salad called *charoset*. The *charoset* symbolizes the mortar of the bricks that the Israelites worked with as slaves.

Charoset for Passover

3 apples, cored and quartered	1 tsp. cinnamon
	Pinch salt
1 c. walnuts	Dash powdered ginger
1/2 c. sweet wine	

Pulse in food processor until chopped.

Finally, the seder participants are able to enjoy the festive meal. Following the meal is dessert, which includes the eating of the *afikomen*. Grace after meals is recited and a special service called Hallel is said. The last part of the seder includes songs and other prayers that God accepts the service.

The seder plate is used and referred to throughout the seder. Even in relatively unobservant homes the original organization of the seder plate remains intact. The *charoset*, green vegetable and salt water, and bitter herbs are all a part of the seder plate. In addition, there is a roasted egg on the seder plate to represent both spring and the cyclical and round nature of life. There is also the shank bone of a lamb. This reminds those present that God spared the Israelites by asking them to put the blood of a lamb on their doorposts to signify that they were Jewish when he enacted the tenth plague of the death of the firstborn Egyptian son. Some families hoping to spread the equality of women in Judaism include an orange on their seder plate. This is because there is a famous rabbi who once said that women belong in positions of power in Judaism just as oranges belong on a seder plate.

Although the preparation of most of the aspects of the seder plate is relatively simple, assembling the *charoset* is involved and greatly varied. Depending on the mood and origin of the cook, *charoset* can be made with a multitude of ingredients. It is usually a comprised of some sort of fruit, nuts, and wine or grape juice. Egyptian *charoset* contains raisins and dates, while Italian *charoset* features chestnut paste, poppy seeds, walnuts, almonds, pine nuts, and brandy. Eastern European *charoset* is simply made with apples, nuts, and sweet wine. Persian Jews make their *charoset* with dates, pistachio, yellow raisins, apples, pomegranate, banana, orange, sweet red wine, cayenne pepper, and cardamom, and Yemenites make theirs with dates, raisins, pomegranate, almonds, and walnuts.

The Pesach seder itself is a true feast that many people begin to prepare many days in advance. Gefilte fish is a staple as a first course at Ashkenazi seders, primarily because of how well it goes with the horseradish. Additionally, matzah ball soup is commonly served with matzah balls not made in the common way with matzah meal, but with fresh ground matzah. Many Ashkenazi cooks also make a special Passover brisket that is prepared in a similar way to other briskets, but with kosher for Passover ingredients. Some people cook the brisket with a large matzah ball and allow the matzah ball to soak in the flavors of the meat and sauce. Sephardi Jews, on the other hand, usually serve some sort of roast lamb dish, in order to remind those present of the Passover lamb. Some Sephardi Jews will alternately make a veal dish, often with artichokes.

Side dishes on Passover usually fall under two categories. One category is foods made with matzah and Passover-related products, and the other category is foods made without them. Although Passover has many restrictions on foods, there are many things that can be eaten and enjoyed just like the rest of the year. The Ashkenazi seder usually includes a potato dish as a side, particularly because it is the only starch other than matzah that is acceptable on Passover. Additionally, many people opt to make either sweet or savory kugels with kosher for Passover egg noodles. Vegetable side dishes are often made with spring vegetables such as artichokes, fava beans, asparagus, or zucchini.

Passover desserts have the reputation of being tough and redolent with the taste of matzah. Coconut macaroons are a popular dessert because they do not require any nonkosher for Passover ingredients. Additionally, many people choose to make flourless tortes on Passover because they too do not require any nonkosher for Passover ingredients. However there are also many desserts that are made only on Passover that include matzah meal, cake meal, and potato starch. There are a myriad of cookbooks and recipe collections that give recipes for kosher for Passover brownies, cookies, cakes, cobblers, and fruit crisps. One popular dessert is *kamish* bread, which is a Jewish type of biscotti made with eggs, matzah meal, sugar, baking soda, and cinnamon, chocolate, fruit preserves, and raisins.

Passover Macaroons

1 1/4 c. sugar	3 egg whites
3/4 c. water	3 c. grated coconut

Preheat oven to 325 degrees F. Make an Italian meringue by cooking sugar and water in a small saucepan until it reaches the soft ball stage (238 degrees F). Meanwhile, beat egg whites with an electric mixer until stiff peaks form. Continue mixing and gradually pour in syrup mixture. Fold in coconut. Drop with two spoons onto a parchment-covered or greased cookie sheet. Bake about 12 minutes and transfer immediately onto wire rack. Macaroons will harden as they cool.

Passover Sponge Cake

With no flour or leavening agent this cake can be made kosher for Passover.

5 eggs, separated	juice and zest of 1/2 lemon
1 c. sugar	1 c. potato starch

Preheat oven to 350. In a large bowl beat egg yolks, sugar, and lemon. In a separate bowl, beat egg whites until stiff peaks form. Fold whites into yolks. Add potato starch and fold gently. Bake for 45 minutes until done.

Meals during the week of Passover are always an event because the holiday necessitates that every meal is prepared instead of bought or eaten out. Although some kosher restaurants in large cities convert before the holiday in order to be kosher for Passover, most families eat all of their meals at home.

Breakfast on Passover is an event in many homes. Although some people may just enjoy yogurt and fruit, many people create elaborate dishes with different combinations of matzah and eggs. One popular Ashkenazi Passover breakfast is matzah *brei,* which is matzah soaked in warm water, coated in eggs, and then fried in a pan with vegetable oil. It is topped with cinnamon and sugar, applesauce, honey, sour cream, and jam, or a combination of salt, pepper, garlic, and onion powder. Another popular Passover breakfast is apple or other fruit fritters. These matzah meal fruity pancakes may be enjoyed with cinnamon and sugar or kosher for Passover syrup and are extremely popular among small children. Some people make Passover rolls or bagels, which tend to be quite hard, but are palatable with cream cheese or preserves. Finally, some people may make a simple omelet or other egg breakfast dish.

Lunches on Passover are relatively uneventful for those who have the week off of work or school, since any number of light foods that are kosher for Passover may be made. Jewish businesses and schools almost always have the week of Passover as a vacation week because of the complications the holiday presents. However, for those who go about their daily business on the *hol ha moed* days of Passover, lunch can be somewhat of a challenge, because the foods that are eaten on Passover do not generally travel well. Though some may simply take leftovers from the seders, others make sandwiches out of matzah or bring salads, meats, yogurt, and other bits of kosher for Passover food.

Dinners during the week of Passover vary from household to household. Many people will make matzah pizza, which is simply a piece of matzah covered in sauce and melted cheese. Also, some make matzah lasagna or will make egg noodles with kosher for Passover tomato sauce. Sephardi Jews make a variety of different vegetable patties, including ones with leeks, zucchini, potatoes, and carrots. Turkish Jews often enjoy a dish called *mina.* It is a hearty matzah *brei* stuffed with spinach and meat and often served with hard-boiled eggs. The last two days of Passover are also considered holidays, and the food eaten on those days is similar to the food eaten at the seder and during the rest of the week.

Though eating matzah outside of the seders is not required, people tend to use it as a substitute for grains in a multitude of dishes. Throughout the week it is common to hear complaints about the overabundance of eggs, potatoes, and of course, matzah. It is noteworthy to mention that fish, chicken, beef, potatoes, and all vegetables and fruits are permissible on Passover and may be cooked as matzah-free dishes, just as one would cook them during the rest of the year.

SHAVUOT

Shavuot, known in non-Jewish circles as the Pentecost, is the last of the three pilgrimage holidays. Agriculturally, it commemorates the time when the first fruits were harvested and brought to the Temple and is known as *Hag ha-Bikkurim* (the Festival of the First Fruits). Historically, Shavuot marks and celebrates the time in which God gave the Torah to the Jewish people. It was at this time they accepted all of the commandments upon themselves. It is a holiday that has observances that originate from the Torah and occurred as part of the wandering of the Israelites through the desert. The name of the holiday literally means "weeks" and is the culmination of the seven-week period between the second day of Passover and the day immediately proceeding Shavuot. It is said that it took this long for the Israelites to reach the spot (Mount Sinai) on their travel from Egypt where they would receive the Torah. Shavuot is two days long in the Diaspora and only one day long in Israel.

It is customary to eat dairy meals on Shavuot. Though there are no places where this is written as a commandment, one will find that in most traditional homes dairy is exclusively served. There are differing reasons given for this. One is that it is commonly repeated in the Torah that Israel was a land "flowing with milk and honey"; dairy products are eaten on Shavuot to mark this. According to another view, it is because the Israelites had just received the Torah (and the dietary laws therein) and did not have the time or resources to understand how to prepare and serve meat properly.

Any foods that include copious amounts of cheese and other dairy products are popular on Shavuot. It is common to make fish as a main course for this holiday because it is a substantial entrée that is not considered meat. Also, many Americans make pasta and cheese dishes on Shavuot, such as baked ziti, lasagna, and others. Dairy kugels are popular, as are cheese platters. The two most common foods served on Shavuot, however, are blintzes and cheesecake.

Blintzes are an Ashkenazi type of crepe that are either filled with fruit or cheese. Although many people buy frozen blintzes, there are many others who make their own. The crepe dough is made with flour, sugar, eggs, butter, and milk and is prefried in vegetable oil. A cheese filling is commonly made with any combination of cream cheese, sour cream, sugar, eggs, and vanilla. The pancakes are filled with the cheese filling, browned on both sides, and then served with sour cream or a fruit sauce. Alternatively, many cooks make blintz soufflé. The blintzes are arranged in a casserole dish and then smothered with a sour cream or cream cheese sauce that includes more butter and sugar. The dish is then baked and topped with a fruit sauce.

Cheese Blintzes

Bletlach (Leaves)

1 c. flour	1/4 tsp salt
1 c. water	2 TBSP melted butter
4 eggs, beaten	

Filling

1/2 lb. cottage cheese	2 TBSP sugar
1/2 lb. farmers cheese	pinch salt
2 egg yolks	

Make leaves by mixing flour, water, eggs and salt. Mix until smooth. Allow batter to rest 20–30 minutes. Brush a small nonstick skillet with melted butter and pour about 2 ounces of crepe batter onto pan. Pour excess back into batter. Cook until lightly brown and then flip. The first one is always ugly.

For filling combine all ingredients. Place an ice-cream scoop of filling in each crepe and roll like an egg roll or burrito. The blintzes can be chilled at this point.

For service, bake uncovered in buttered casserole at 350 degrees for about 35 minutes.

Cheesecake is the quintessential Shavuot dessert. Any variation on cheesecake that any American cook would create is made on Shavuot. Chocolate, chocolate chip, strawberry, peanut butter, oreo, and vanilla are common flavors; however, Jewish American cooks are likely to add many other exotic flavorings to the basic cheesecake recipe.

JEWISH LIFE-CYCLE EVENTS

Just as the holidays of the calendar year are remarkably tied with foods, so too are the Jewish life-cycle events. This should not come as a surprise; since food is so integral to Jewish American culture it would only make sense that the major events in a Jew's lifetime are marked in some way with food. All life-cycle events, whether large or small, are accompanied by a meal of some sort and a variety of blessings and prayers.

Birth

According to Jewish tradition the birth of a child is one of the most joyous occasions possible because it is the beginning of not only a new life, but also of a new Jewish life. The birth of either a boy or a girl are surely festive occasions; however, the two are accompanied by different naming ceremonies. It is traditional that the child is not formally given his or her name until at least eight days after the birth because of the fragile nature of the early days of life. After eight healthy days, the naming ceremonies may occur.

It is almost universal American Jewish practice to have a naming ceremony and a Brith Milah, or *bris* for a baby boy, despite the observance level of the family. This is a ritual in which the boy is circumcised and enters into the Jewish community, and therefore receives his name and his identity. The *bris* is an occasion that is usually attended by family, friends, and other members of the community and is usually performed by a *moyel* (someone who is specially trained to do circumcisions).

Though the parents of the boy are usually nervous, the *bris* is an extremely joyous occasion and is always accompanied by a festive yet casual meal. The only food that is traditional to serve at a *bris* is *nahit*, a boiled chickpea dish. The roundness of the chickpeas are meant to symbolize fertility and the cyclical nature of life. The meal that people enjoy after a *bris* varies by region; however, it is common to serve bagels, cream cheese, smoked fish, and an assortment of salads.

Baby girls are also not traditionally named until after eight healthy days; however, the naming ceremony for a girl is not as traditional nor as established as the Brith Milah. Most people who have a naming ceremony for a new daughter wait much longer than eight days for the official naming ceremony and think of the ritual as merely symbolic. The naming ceremony for a girl usually takes place in the synagogue on Shabbat and is performed by the rabbi. Often the family hosts a kiddush luncheon following services.

Bar and Bat Mitzvah

The coming of age ceremony is the next major event in a Jew's life. The bar mitzvah (for a boy) and bat mitzvah (for a girl) is the time in which the 13-year-old adolescent enters into Jewish adulthood. It is marked by being called to the Torah and reciting a special blessing before the community and is the time in which the teen announces to the public that he or she is ready to take on more (or all of) the commandment required of a Jewish adult.

Elaborate bar mitzvah Kiddush luncheon. Courtesy of Rabbi Moshe and Meira Saks.

Although the major event of a bar or bat mitzvah is when the boy or girl is called to the Torah, in American Jewish society the main event has, in most cases, become the party. There are no foods particular to bar or bat mitzvah celebrations, and the celebratory meal following it can be anything from an extended kiddush luncheon to a lavish formal black tie affair. Usually catered, bar and bat mitzvah parties may include anything from a simple meal of bagels and cream cheese to an abundant feast of filet mignon for the adults and chicken fingers, pasta bars, stir fry stations, popcorn stands, and more for the kids. There is always a palpable air of excitement and expectation at a bar or bat mitzvah because of the promise the event holds for the future of the bar or bat mitzvah boy or girl.

Weddings

Jewish weddings involve a great deal of ceremony, formalities, and sheer joy. There are countless traditions surrounding weddings; however, the most important is that the groom gives the bride a ring and that there is a document called a *ketubbah* to protect the woman's rights in case of abandonment or other marital troubles. Also, the bride and groom traditionally fast on the day of their wedding because the Jewish wedding day is likened to Yom Kippur. The first food or drink they have is wine that is blessed during the ceremony, and they are then able to eat some food as they share a few private moments immediately following the ceremony.

It is a commandment that those present at a wedding must rejoice with the bride and groom by keeping them happy and feeding them. It is for this reason that an integral part of the Jewish wedding is the wedding meal, or *seudah*. Although there are no traditional Jewish American wedding foods there are particularly customary at a wedding. Jewish American weddings are often catered sumptuous meals, and are almost always served as meat meals, not dairy. There is a special *birkat hamazon* recited at the end of the wedding during which there are seven blessings recited over two cups of wine. The cups are combined and then given to the bride and groom to drink as a token of good luck.

Funerals and Mourning

As in many other cultures, death and mourning in Jewish American society is met with a great deal of sadness. When one loses someone particularly close to them (a mother, father, sister, brother, or child) they enter into a period called shiva for seven days. During this period they are in a deep state of mourning, and the community usually comes together to provide meals and other support. There are a number of prohibitions for those in shiva, and people observe these commandments in different ways, depending on their observance level. The only true food customs related to funerals and death are that upon returning home from a cemetery those in mourning customarily eat a hard-boiled egg. The egg represents the roundness of life and the chance of renewal of life and spirit at all times. The eating of the egg, like many other customs surrounding death and mourning, is an action that reaffirms faith in life and in God.

7

Diet and Health

Because Jews in America are both a cultural group and members of a religion with clear dietary laws as a defining characteristic, for religious and nonreligious Jewish Americans alike, the Jewish dietary laws are central to conceptions of diet and health. Observing the laws—or straying from them—makes a strong statement about identity. Just as *peyos* (long side locks), a yarmulke, or a wig may be a public expression of one's identity as an observant Jewish American, so is adherence to dietary laws. Conversely, just as a Jewish American who identifies as culturally but not religiously Jewish may not cover his head, he may not follow the laws at all or may select to follow only some of them, eschewing pork, for example, but not hesitating to follow a meat dinner with a slice of cheesecake.

Kashrut, Jewish dietary law, is not only a religious practice but is one tied to perceptions of health and the body as well. While chemistry, biology, and physiology may tell us that beef and pork are very similar in composition and nutrition, for example, one cannot ignore the psychology of the laws, in which an observant Jewish American may be as disgusted at the thought of eating pork as a typical Jewish or non-Jewish American would be when invited to eat a plate of live grubs.

KASHRUT

For observant Jews the dietary laws define all aspects of food preparation, consumption, and enjoyment. The Jewish dietary laws are one of the major ways that Jews separate themselves from other religions, creating a Jewish community. Jews have kept kosher ever since the origin of the religion, and

Kosher food section in a supermarket. Courtesy of Rachel Saks.

the nature of that observance has remained relatively unchanged. Kashrut is so sacred that when an American Jew makes the decision (or is born into the decision) to keep kosher he or she is making a decision to separate him- or herself in all arenas in which food is involved.

However, there is a rich kosher food culture. The kosher food industry is hugely popular and is becoming more diverse every year. Currently there are over 98,000 kosher certified products in America that are bought by over 1,100,000 strictly kosher consumers.[1] In addition, many kosher products are part of the mainstream market. Someone who is not kosher may not even realize that the potato chips, snack cake, or soft drink she or he is eating is a certified kosher product. But a Jew following the laws of kashrut would be sure to check the label for the kosher symbol.

The laws of kashrut are filled with details and seemingly endless differing opinions; however, the laws are a discipline in holiness and define for many people a way of life.

Why Kashrut?

Many scholars (Jewish and non-Jewish) and Jews have wondered for thousands of years about the purpose of kashrut. For the most devoutly faithful

Jews one need not look farther than the Torah, the first five books of the Bible and the first and most important tome on Jewish law, for the answer. The Torah details many of the laws of kashrut, and although it does not provide a reason for the laws, it is enough for many Jews to know that kashrut is the word of God, as recorded in the Torah, and therefore must be observed. The reason to observe the laws, then, is simply because God said that one should observe the laws.

Chapter 11 of Leviticus is entirely devoted to the laws of kashrut. Here is an excerpt:

The Lord spoke to Moses and Aaron. . . . These are the creatures that you may eat from among all the land animals: any animal that has true hoofs, with clefts through the hoofs, and chews the cud—such you may eat. The following however, of those that either chew the cud or have true hooves, you shall not eat . . . they are unclean for you. These you may eat of all that live in water: anything in water . . . that has fins and scales . . . but anything in water that has no fins or scales . . . they are an abomination for you. . . . The following you should abominate among the birds.

The text goes on to forbid a number of different birds, most insects, and a menagerie of other creatures that are forbidden. The text also recounts that anything that touches any of the forbidden animals is also forbidden, and that one may not eat an animal that is generally permitted if it is found dead. Additionally, a later section recounts that one may not boil a kid in its mothers milk (Deut 14:21). Clearly there is no reason given here for these prohibitions; however, for those who believe that God's word must be followed a reason is unimportant.

The earliest commentators on the Torah struggled with how to translate this cryptic code of dietary law into a set of rules that could be followed daily. Sages from the period of the Mishnah and Talmud argued and discussed endlessly the particulars of the laws and how they should be practically followed; however, they rarely questioned the reasoning behind the laws. It was not until the medieval period, a time in which Jewish adherence to laws of the Bible that the Christians considered irrelevant was challenged, that scholars began to give possible reasons for observing kashrut. Maimonides, a well-respected Jewish-Spanish rabbi and scholar, wrote, "I maintain that the food forbidden by the law is unwholesome. There is nothing among the forbidden foods whose injurious character is doubted except for pork and fat. But also in these cases is the doubt justified." Put simply, Maimonides believed that the Jews followed kashrut because it is healthy. Various examples follow. For example, shellfish is highly perishable, and pork may carry the trichina worm, a potential cause of illness in humans. While these characteristics may be true, they do not answer the question completely.

For years, scholars have been theorizing on the roots of kosher law. Why is pig forbidden but not cow? Why shellfish but not fish? Why not combine meat and dairy? While a religious Jew may answer, "Because it is written that way in the Torah," others seek to understand the frame of mind of these early Jews. Anthropologist Marvin Harris argues that the laws of kashrut were founded based on practical considerations of the time.[2] For example, cows, sheep, and goats give both milk and meat and are kosher. Pigs are resource-intensive, giving flesh upon slaughter but no usable milk through their life span and became *treyf* (forbidden). Anthropologist Mary Douglas makes a famous argument that foods that are taboo to Jews are those that do not fit into early Jewish ideas of the natural order of the world.[3] Shellfish, for example, live in the ocean but do not swim. That makes them an anomaly, unnatural in this framework and therefore forbidden. Similarly, young mammals are meant to suckle milk from their mother. To cook them in it—and by extension, to combine meat and dairy—is to corrupt this natural order in the biblical-era worldview, Douglas suggests.

For most Jews, both secular and observant, the laws of kashrut are confusing and seemingly random. There are commentators, however, that give more theological reasons for the observance of kashrut. Many scholars, both present and past, believe that the observance of kashrut allows Jews to enjoy a deep level of holiness. The sections of the Torah in which the laws of kashrut are found are actually solely devoted to holiness. Traditionally, kashrut is thought of as a spiritual discipline, one that is symbolic of the struggle between the good inclination in human beings and the evil inclination in human beings. Observing kashrut is a means through which people can reach the spiritual by heeding the physical.

One twentieth-century rabbi explains,

Eating is one of the important functions of life. It begins as a biological act, a means of satisfying hunger. When we invite a friend for dinner, a new dimension is added to eating; it becomes a social act. It helps to cement friendship. When a meal takes place in connection with the joy of observance of a commandment, it becomes a solemn act that helps add significance to an occasion. On the Sabbath, or even more, on Passover at the Seder, eating becomes a religious act, an act of worship, with the table becoming an altar of God.[4]

There is another reasoning behind the laws of kashrut, which suggests that their purpose is to teach a special respect for life. Although Jews are permitted to eat meat, they must do so only if the meat has been slaughtered according to Jewish law, designed for humane slaughter, in order to prevent a cavalier attitude to all forms of life.

Finally, many American Jews who follow some form of kashrut but are liberal in their approach to theology observe kashrut simply because it is part of Jewish custom. Those wishing to be part of a larger Jewish community and feel a connection to history will often observe kashrut as a nod to all the Jews of the past who did the same. In a similar way, some Jewish Americans keep kosher homes but loosen the rules when dining out, while others make kosher or kosher-style meals for Jewish holidays to observe customs but do not regularly observe the laws of kashrut.

KOSHER ANIMALS

There are a number of domesticated and undomesticated animals that are kosher. These are limited to cattle, sheep, goats, yak, buffalo, and any animal in the deer family. There are certain laws that pertain to animals that were considered by the rabbis as undomesticated that do not apply to those that are domesticated, and there are a number of marks that one can check for if one is not sure if a particular undomesticated animal is kosher. Particularly, any mammal that does not chew its cud and have cloven hooves is nonkosher.

The Torah is not as specific about the consumption of birds as it is about the consumption of meat. Instead, it explains that all birds of prey are nonkosher and lists all of the species of birds that are forbidden. This list of 24 does not include chickens, turkeys, ducks, geese, pigeons, and pheasants, which makes those animals permissible.

Fish is a category that is considered completely separate from chicken and beef, and any sea creature that has both fins and scales is allowable. This naturally leaves out all seafood, such as lobster, shrimp, and scallops. Some fish such as monkfish, which do not have scales, are not kosher. Also, all insects with the exception of a few species of locusts are not kosher.

The Slaughter of Kosher Animals

All meat and birds that are permitted must be slaughtered in a prescribed manner called *schitah*. This is a special way of killing the animal that allows for maximum spillage of blood and an extremely quick death, with the goal of being a more humane slaughter. *Schitah* is performed by a well-trained and licensed professional referred to as a *shochet,* or slaughterer. The *shochet* wields a long and sharp knife and cuts the trachea and the esophagus of the animal in one clean motion.

Maimonides explained that killing animals in this specified way is actually a way of fulfilling the commandment of preventing cruelty to animals. Some commentators explain that certain verses in the Torah could lead one to believe that man was not originally intended to eat meat and that doing so is a compromise with God. The rules behind *schitah* and kashrut, therefore, show

Traditional knife (*chalaf*) used by the kosher butcher to slaughter an animal.
© J. Susan Cole Stone.

a restraint from eating certain parts of the animal that are considered dirty or inhumane to eat, such as the blood.

The laws of *schitah* are very specific, and although all of the details will not be given here, some highlights are important. The knife that is used by the *shochet* must be razor sharp and perfectly smooth, since any dents or nicks would tear the flesh of the animal and cause unnecessary pain. Before performing the *schitah* the *shochet* recites the blessing, "Blessed are you, God, Ruler of the universe, who has sanctified us with His commandments and commanded us to perform *schitah*." The cut is then made horizontally across the esophagus and trachea. There are a number of rules that the *shochet* must adhere to that are listed and discussed in the Talmud. The *shochet* must not delay or pause the slaughtering, he may not chop or strike the animal, he may not burrow or insert the blade, he may not cut out any parts of the animal, and he may not injure or cut the esophagus or trachea with any other cuts during the slaughtering.

Inspecting the Animal

After slaughtering the animal the *shochet* must thoroughly examine it to determine if there any blemishes or pathological conditions that would render the animal not kosher. The *shochet* checks for a number of conditions that would suggest that the animal was close to death or very sick before being slaughtered. In the United States, this would be in addition to the inspection from the U.S. Department of Agriculture required by law. If one of the defects that the *shochet* checks for is present, the animal is rendered nonkosher, or *treyf*. However, it should be noted that while the *shochet* needs to inspect all animals that are slaughtered for adhesions, he only needs to check for other possible defects in cattle that are suspicious for one reason or another.

There are multiple types of adhesions that make cattle nonkosher; however, there are some that are inconsequential. The coloration and texture of the lungs is also important. If there is a reason to suspect a problem in any part of the animal, then the skull, spinal cord, ribs, legs, digestive system, throat, stomach, intestines, liver, gallbladder, pancreas, and spleen must also be inspected. The inspection laws that apply to cattle do not apply to birds; however, there are similar laws for inspecting all types of fowl.

Preparing the Animal

To be considered kosher an animal must undergo a thorough process of fat and blood removal and of soaking and salting. "*Porging*," in Hebrew *nikur*, is the process of removing forbidden fat, residual blood, and veins. Much of the *porging* is done by the *shochet*, because when the neck is sliced most of the blood drains from the animal. However, special attention must be paid to certain veins and sacs that carry excess blood.

Today the butcher still carries out part of the process. There are multiple reasons that kosher meat must contain only trace amounts of blood. In general in the Torah blood is thought of as a substance that has the ability to render anything impure. Blood symbolizes life and death, and to observant Jews the consumption of blood would be both brutalizing to the once living, breathing animal and brutalizing to the one who consumes the blood, because it is a marker of death.

In cattle and sheep there are various areas of fat that are not considered kosher and therefore must be removed from the animal before the process of salting and soaking. Any fat that is only loosely connected to the flesh must be removed, and any fat that is not surrounded by muscle must be removed. The sciatic nerve in the back of the animal must be removed. This is extremely difficult to do, even for an expert, so kosher animals are usually butchered without the hindquarters. The hindquarters, although the animal is slaughtered in the kosher manner, are sold separately as *treyf* meat.

After the *porging* process the animal is rinsed and soaked in water for half an hour in order to remove any excess blood. Some rabbis also say this is necessary in order to soften the meat and allow for the later salting to be successful. The process of soaking is one that must be timed well. It cannot take place too long after the slaughtering, and if the meat is soaked too long it will no longer be considered kosher.

After the meat is soaked, the final step is the salting. Salting draws out even more blood from the meat. All kosher meat must be salted liberally and must be covered completely in salt. The salt should be a medium grain salt to ensure that it neither dissolves too quickly nor rolls off the animal. After an hour of salting, the meat is considered kosher.

DAIRY PRODUCTS

Some religious American Jews believe that all dairy products, including milk and butter, need to be specifically marked as kosher. The reason for this is a fear that some nonkosher substance will mix in with the milk by mistake, even though that is highly unlikely because of food regulations in the United States and elsewhere. Nevertheless, many observant Jews will only consume dairy products that have been watched from the moment of milking until the packaging process.

There is a particular difficulty with cheese when it comes to kashrut. Rennet, a common curdling agent in cheese, is actually a product extracted from the walls of a calf's stomach. In ancient times cheese was actually forbidden for this reason because it was in fact a mixture of meat and milk. However, according to some authorities the use of rennet does not affect the kashrut of the cheese because rennet no longer has the status of food, as it is used in a way that is so far from its original form. Furthermore, in America cheese making is regulated by the Pure Food and Drug Law, which requires that a list of the ingredients be readily available to the consumer. In the case of hard cheeses, the rennet is so thoroughly treated that most authorities allow it. There are rennet substitutes available that are used in the production of vegetarian and other kosher cheeses.

Separation of Meat and Milk

Jewish Americans who keep kosher have little to do with any of the processes described in the last section, other than buying meat from a kosher butcher. However, there are many aspects of kashrut that the kosher consumer busies him- or herself with on a daily basis. One of the most basic rules of kashrut is that meat may not be eaten with any dairy product, and this is something that the Jewish American cook needs to be very wary of.

For the purposes of kashrut, a dairy product is any product that contains a derivative from milk in any form, even a somewhat foreign and chemically altered one, such as lecithin or casein. This prohibition comes from the section of Deuteronomy that says, "You shall not boil a kid in its mother's milk" (14:21). The rabbis explain that this prohibition includes not eating any animal (other than fish) with milk and that a kid is specifically mentioned in the text of the Torah because cooking a young goat in the milk of its mother was a prevalent custom of the time.

Neither the Torah nor the Talmud give any explanation as to why it is impermissible to eat milk and meat together. Maimonides suggests that this prohibition signifies God's (and the Jewish people's) disgust over the Canaanite custom of eating an animal in its own mother's milk. There were also some medieval Jewish doctors and scholars who believed it to be unhealthy for the body to combine milk and meat. Modern scholars suggest that this prohibition again marks how the laws of kashrut are in place to ensure respect for life and animals and to prevent cruelty and callousness.

The Waiting Period

Not only is it forbidden to eat meat and milk together, it is also forbidden to eat one right after the other, such as a dairy dessert after a meat meal. The reason for a waiting period is that food leaves lingering taste in one's mouth and in one's body that has the chance to remain for a long time. Also, particles of food, particularly meat, have a good chance of getting stuck in one's teeth. People wait different amounts of time according to different authorities; however, after eating meat people wait anywhere from one hour to six hours before consuming any dairy. After having dairy, however, people wait anywhere from five minutes to one hour. It is suggested to wait longer to eat dairy after having meat than the other way around because it is thought that the flavor of the meat remains in the mouth and body longer than the flavors of dairy.

Keeping Meat and Milk Separate

There are a number of precautions that Jewish Americans who keep kosher homes make to ensure that they do not ever mix meat and milk. First, it is necessary to have two sets of dishes: one for meat meals, and one for milk meals. This goes beyond simply having two sets of plates. It means having two sets of knives, cutting boards, pots and pans, silverware, mugs, table linens, cooking utensils, mixing bowls, baking pans, and more. Those who keep a stricter version of kashrut will not allow their meat and milk dishes to ever come in contact with one another, therefore storing them in separate areas of the kitchen. Some homes and most kosher institutions such as schools and hospitals have entirely separate kitchens.

The sink is a very difficult area to manage when it comes to kashrut. Some authorities say that the only way to deal with the sink is to either have two of them (or a sink with two sides and one faucet) or to simply use basins of water on the top of the counter. Since it is difficult for people to have two sinks and challenging to use basins, especially in a small kitchen or an apartment, there are a number of ways of circumventing the problem of the sink.

The most liberal way of dealing with the problem of the sink is to use it for only meat dishes or only dairy dishes at one time, and to switch on and off. This is a practice that many people use and is deemed acceptable by many rabbis. Often, however, people choose to view their sink as nonkosher and use a separate mat and sink rack for meat and dairy. This ensures that the dishes only touch the rack and never the sink, since it is impossible to make sure that milk and meat do not mix in the surface of the sink. It is also customary to have separate sponges, one for meat and one for dairy; however, there are varying levels to this observance.

It follows from the necessity of having a kosher sink that there is also an issue with draining boards. Those who are most observant use two draining boards, one for meat and one for dairy. Others use their one draining board for only meat or dairy at one time, while still others mix meat and milk dishes on the draining board.

The dishwasher is another area of conflict in the Jewish American kitchen. As can be assumed by now, those who adhere to kashrut in the strictest manner possible either have two dishwashers or use the dishwasher at all times for either meat or dairy (and then always hand wash the other). It is also common, however, for Jewish Americans to not wash meat and milk dishes together and to run a full cycle between the washing of meat and dairy dishes. Still, other people choose not to worry about the dishwasher and use it for milk and meat simultaneously.

The main battle between dairy and meat foods and utensils takes place on the cooking range, where boiling pots are ready to overflow at any time and utensils are likely to be confused. Since it is extremely rare for a domestic kitchen to have two cooking ranges, it is up to the cook to either not cook dairy and meat at the same time, or to be extra cautious while doing so. Some people take extra precaution when cooking milk and meat by putting up a temporary barrier, such as a cookie sheet, to ward off any accidental mixing of meat and dairy.

The oven is also a difficult area for the domestic Jewish American kosher cook, since it is just as rare to have two ovens as it is to have two stoves. Most people who observe kashrut would not cook meat and dairy together in the same oven because there is concern that the odors of the meat, for example, would penetrate the dairy. In some circles it is customary to wait 24 hours between using the oven for dairy cooking after meat, and vice versa.

Milk and Meat at the Same Table

It is permissible for two people to eat at the same table, one eating a meat meal and the other eating a dairy meal. However, many people use some sort of marker to remind themselves and those around them of the separation between the two. Thus, separate tablecloths or placemats are commonly used. Also, a separate loaf of bread and separate salt and pepper shakers must be used.

The Unintentional Mixing of Meat and Milk

Even the most careful and observant person will come across times in which milk and meat mix by accident. This can occur in any area of the kitchen at any time and often serves as a reminder of how difficult the laws of kashrut are to follow. If everyone in a house is not aware of all of the designations of meat and dairy in a kitchen before using it, then it is likely that objects will become mixed. One must have an intimate knowledge of one's kitchen and ensure that objects and areas are properly labeled, perhaps, in order to ensure that one's children's friends or one's relatives do not tamper with the balance of meat and milk in the kitchen.

There are two basic things that one must ask when an accidental mixing occurs. One is about the temperature of the food or items mixed, and the other is about the volume of the substance (milk, perhaps) in relation to the volume that was mixed with the incorrect substance (meat).

The basic rule of thumb that almost all kosher Jewish Americans adhere to is that if both foods or utensils are cold, then both remain kosher. As long as the two things are in contact for less than 24 hours then they simply must be separated and rinsed. Utensils that are mixed need to be not only separated, but thoroughly cleaned.

Complications arise when one or both of the foods or items that are mixed are hot. If, for example, a piece of meat falls into a pot of milk and both are hot, both become forbidden. If, however, one of them is hot and the other cold the rules differ. If the lower item is hot and the item that falls in is cold, then both are considered forbidden. If, however, the lower substance is cold and the item that is dropped is hot, then both items are permissible. There are some who say in this case that the surface of the meat must be trimmed to ensure that no milk penetrated its surface.

There is a concept in the Talmud when it comes to many matters of kashrut known as *bateil b'shishim,* which loosely translated asks the question of whether or not one item is 60 times the volume of another. Generally in kashrut if one item is less than 60 times the volume of another then at least one of those things can still be considered kosher. If, for example, a piece of meat falls into hot milk but is immediately removed, the milk is still kosher because of this principle. The meat, however, is not kosher, because it is assumed that the milk is well over 60 times its volume. There are also lengthy discussions over whether or not the stirring of a meat soup or stew that has an accidental drop of milk in it is acceptable. There are many specifics for these issues and a multitude of opinions.

By defining, debating, and examining these issues, American Jews express both their faith and their identity.

Milk and Meat Dishes

As has already been explained, it is necessary in a kosher kitchen to have separate dishes for meat and dairy. Certain materials are considered to be either acceptable for use with meat or dairy meals, while others are able to be made kosher if an accident occurs. Because glass is not porous, glass dishes are considered pareve, which means that they are neither meat nor diary. There are some people who opt to use glass dishes and glass serveware in their kosher kitchens so that they only need one set; however, this is not the practice among more observant individuals. Any earthenware or plastic dish or object is not able to be made kosher again once it is previously made nonkosher; however, metal materials and utensils are able to be koshered.

Kashering Dishes

Just as areas of the kitchen will likely come into contact with either meat or dairy when they are not supposed to, so too will dishes, pots, and pans. There are a set of rules for rekashering (making items kosher again) dishes if they have been compromised in any way. It is important to note that in a situation with cold on cold contact, such as a cold turkey sandwich on a meat plate, there is no need to rekasher the plate and the sandwich may still be eaten.

If a metal meat pot is mistakenly used for a diary dish then it, and any other metal object, may be thoroughly cleansed by dropping it into boiling water. The utensils, pots, or dishes should be thoroughly clean to start with and should not be used for 24 hours prior to when the koshering will take place. The utensil or pot is then immersed in boiling water and rinsed in cold water. If an object is too big to immerse in a pot of water, then it is permissible to dip one side and then the other, or to simply pour boiling water from another vessel over the entire surface of the object that is being koshered.

Most authorities say that it is impermissible to kasher an object that is not made entirely of metal, such as a knife with a wooden handle, because the wood is not able to be made kosher again. However, it should be noted that it is common among American Jews to kasher utensils such as these as long as the part that mainly has the contact with the food is able to be koshered.

Pareve Foods

Although laws on dairy and meat make up the bulk of the laws of kashrut, there are a multitude of foods that are considered neither dairy nor meat. All produce, nuts, grains, eggs, and fish are considered pareve, which means that they are neither dairy nor meat foods. Pareve foods may be eaten with either a meat or a milk meal. Some Jewish American cooks choose to have a third set of dishes and utensils for all pareve meals. It should also be noted that vegetables, for example, that contain no meat or dairy but were cooked in a meat pot, are not considered meat. One may eat the vegetables and eat cheese immediately after. Also, while fish is considered to be pareve, it may not be combined with meat in any way. This means that if one is having a fish appetizer, for example, one must use separate utensils and separate dishes.

Kashrut and Non-Jews

Wine

There are a number of laws on kashrut that relate to non-Jews and the handling of kosher food. One of the biggest problem areas for many observant Jewish Americans is wine. From earliest times, wine was used by all religions for their worship. It was and remains very common for people of various religions to actually devote some of their wine to their idols. This is not anything that Jews ever did, because idolatry is forbidden in Judaism. It was because of this type of idol worship, however, that the rabbis of the Mishnah decided that Jews should not only not drink non-Jewish wine, they should also not drink any wine that has been handled at any point in production by non-Jews, because they could potentially be idol worshippers and may have consecrated the wine at some point for idol worship. Although this no longer occurs with the production of wine, the prohibition remains.

Extremely observant circles explain the continuation of this prohibition as a preventative measure against intermarriage between Jews and non-Jews in a way. They claim that drinking wine leads to a weakened sense of judgment, and that drinking wine in non-Jewish company may lead to a situation that could eventually lead to romantic attachment. Thus, by barring non-Jewish wine, the rabbis drew the demarcation line indicating to what extent Jews may mix with non-Jewish neighbors. There are actually some restaurants that, keeping in mind their religious clientele, have separate rooms that have Jewish waiters, so that if a table chooses to order a bottle of wine, that wine does not come into contact with non-Jewish hands.

Keeping these strict opinions in mind, there are many more lenient opinions on kosher wine. Much winemaking is fully automated and no human hand comes into contact with the wine from the moment grapes are put into containers and brought to the winery until the wine appears in sealed bottles. Additionally, there are many people who insist that kosher wine be used for religious ceremonies and blessings, but that wine used for other occasions is acceptable.

In the United States the problem of non-Jews handling kosher wine is often solved by boiling the wine. If the wine is boiled before bottling it is considered kosher even if it is handled at any point by a non-Jew.

Food Cooked by Non-Jews

In traditional circles a non-Jew may take part in preparing food in a Jewish kitchen, but the actual cooking must not be done by him or her. This clearly presents a difficulty in America, where Jews make up such a small percentage of the population, and religious Jews an even smaller percentage. There are two reasons for this. One is to be found in a common Jewish principle that states that whoever is not obliged to observe a commandment cannot truly appreciate its significance. Because of this, he or she is unable, in a way, to appreciate the significance of the law and is likely to make a mistake. The other reason is similar to the reason given for the consumption of non-Jewish wine. It is meant to prevent intimate friendships between Jews and non-Jews that might lead to intermarriage.

According to Talmudic law there are three stages of the cooking process. These are lighting the fire, bringing the food into contact with the fire, and allowing the food to become edible due to the fire. In order for food to be considered kosher—and this is particularly relevant in a restaurant or with caterers—a Jew must take part in at least one of these three stages. In res- taurants it is most common for a Jew to simply start the fire by lighting the ovens and stoves and then walk away and let the cooks continue on. Some complications arise with this when one takes into consideration whether the food in question is customarily eaten raw. Non-Jews may prepare foods that are usually eaten raw, such as tomatoes, milk, water, and most fruits. They may also heat up a precooked meal.

Immersion of Utensils

In very observant circles in America, utensils used for eating or preparing food, which have at any time been in the ownership of a non-Jew and which are now owned by a Jew, require immersion at a *mikveh*, a ritual pool, before being used. This immersion is called *tevila*. The traditional explanation of this is that just as a convert to Judaism must undergo immersion in a *mikveh*, so too must a utensil owned by a non-Jew. The utensil is, in a way, converted to Judaism and is uplifted to a new level.

This applies to utensils that were manufactured in a non-Jewish factory and to utensils purchased in a non-Jewish store, even if they were manufactured in a Jewish factory. Utensils merely borrowed from a non-Jew do not require *tevila* (as long as they are otherwise 100 percent kosher), but utensils borrowed from a Jew who has not yet immersed them must be immersed. Only vessels made of gold, silver, iron, steel, copper, tin, brass, lead, glass, Pyrex, Corelle, and crystal require *tevila* with a blessing. Unglazed earthenware, wood, rubber, and plastic utensils require no *tevila*. Corningware, porcelain (china), enam- eled pots, Teflon-coated pans, and aluminum vessels require *tevila* without a

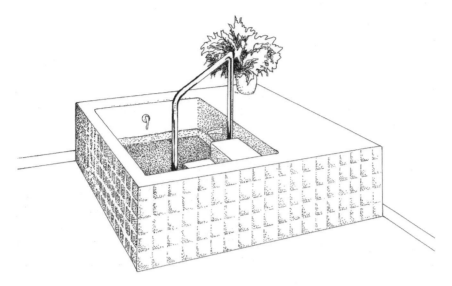

Mikveh for immersing utensils. © J. Susan Cole Stone.

blessing. Disposable aluminum pans require no *tevila*. Some authorities even hold that one should not purchase an appliance if it has direct contact with food and is unable to be immersed, such as a toaster oven.

Before immersion, anything stuck onto the utensil, such as a label or price tag, must be removed. It also must be thoroughly cleaned. When applicable, the following blessing is said before immersion: "Blessed are you, Lord our God, King of the Universe, who has sanctified us with His commandments and has commanded us to immerse utensils." The utensil is then held with a loose grip and with prewetted hands. The utensil is then dipped into the water, and if possible, let loose for a fraction of a second, so that there is a moment when it is completely in contact with the water. Practically, this is a very difficult observance to follow, especially since there are not many *mikvehs* in the United States that are even available to immerse utensils.

BLOOD AND BUGS IN FOOD

As has been made clear, one of the primary issues with kashrut is blood and its symbolic nature. Because blood is a marker for the beauty of life and is considered in all instances impure, one may not eat any food with blood in it. One food that commonly has blood spots is eggs. Although blood spots are uncommon in mass-produced eggs, locally produced and organic eggs are becoming more popular, and these types of eggs have frequent blood spots. Usually the blood is found in the yolk of an egg, although occasionally there may be a spot in the white.

Because the majority of eggs do not have blood spots it is permissible to eat a hard-boiled egg without examining it first. However, if one is taking a raw egg from its shell to use it for frying or baking, it must be inspected. The reason for this is that not to examine an egg in such cases is considered to be deliberately ignoring a possible blood spot, one that could have been detected upon examination. Any time an egg with a blood spot is mixed in with other foods, either hot or cold, both the food and the cooking vessel are rendered nonkosher.

In addition to prohibiting specific mammals, the Torah also prohibits the consumption of all bugs, with the exception of certain types of locusts. Although food may be considered perfectly clean by the health authorities, observant Jews must satisfy themselves that their produce, especially, is clean of all insects and worms. Depending on where food is grown and how it is treated prior to arriving at a grocery store determines what produce must be checked and how it should be checked.

Certain foods are almost always free of insects, while some have a greater tendency to have bugs. Foods like oranges, coconuts, sour apples, bananas, tomatoes, and potatoes seldom have insects or worms in them and do not need to be inspected. However, nearly all green vegetables need to be examined. These include, but are not limited to, cabbage, lettuce, parsley, spinach, celery, asparagus, broccoli, and peas, as well as mushrooms. Dates, figs, walnuts, cherries, apples, berries, peaches, and olives also must be inspected.

All one needs to examine food for bugs or worms is good eyesight and adequate light. With fruit one must check that there are no holes where worms may have entered. There is no special place where worms or insects are found on vegetables, so the whole leaf or vegetable must be thoroughly examined. If an insect or worm is found it is permissible to cut off that piece of the food that the insect touched and eat the rest of it.

Microorganisms and bugs that cannot be seen by the naked eye are obviously acceptable. Since nearly every food is crawling with microorganisms, it is a good thing they are permissible.

SEPARATING CHALLAH

Any bread that one buys from a store must have an appropriate kosher marking on it (a *heksher*); however, one may also make bread or cakes at home from all kosher ingredients. A bread or cake dough made from at least two and a half pounds of flour, which at the time of kneading belongs to a Jewish person, requires separation of *challah*. This means that a piece of the dough (at least the size of an olive) is separated from the rest of the dough and disposed

Various American kosher symbols.

of in some way. The origin of this practice is actually from the Torah, where it says, "Separate the first portion of your kneading as a dough offering. . . . In future generations, give the first of your kneading as an elevated gift to God" (Numbers 15:21). The purpose of this was for the people to thank the high priests with a small offering of bread. Although there are no longer high priests or a Temple, there are some Jews that continue the practice of separating challah in their home. (It should be noted that the traditional Shabbat bread is actually called challah, and that it is common for people to only separate the challah when making the special Shabbat bread.)

The obligations of taking challah applies only to dough that contains flour made from wheat, barley, rye, oats, or spelt, or to a dough-like mixture of these. If there are more than five pounds of flour in the dough then a blessing is said when the piece is separated. The blessing is, "Blessed are you, Lord our God, King of the Universe, who has sanctified us with His commandments and commanded us to separate challah." The challah is taken before the bread is shaped, but after it is kneaded, and it is either burned in the oven or thrown in the trash.

PASSOVER AND KASHRUT

The holiday of Passover provides an entirely new set of problems to deal with when it comes to kashrut. On Passover it is forbidden to eat leaven, which includes wheat, rye, barley, oats and spelt that has not been completely cooked within 18 minutes after coming into contact with water. Many Jewish Americans who are of an Ashkenazi background also avoid rice, corn, peanuts, and legumes. For most observant Jewish Americans it is not enough that these things not be eaten, one must not eat anything that has ever come into contact with these things.

American Jews who are not particularly observant of kashrut laws during the rest of the year often are quite observant of the laws of Passover.

It is very common for observant Jewish Americans to have entire separate sets of milk and meat dishes, utensils, and pots and pans for use during Passover. This eliminates the need to kasher dishes; however, one must still go through the process of kashering the kitchen itself. If there are utensils that need to be kashered, the same rules that apply to kashering utensils during the rest of the year apply here.

Kashering the kitchen entails a number of things. It is customary to cover the countertops, either with aluminum foil or a custom-made covering of plexiglass or some other material. The oven must be thoroughly cleaned and then set either to self-clean or broil for a number of hours. The stove top is heated until it is red hot, and some people even go as far as pouring boiling water on the floor to ensure that it is kosher as well. Finally, cabinets and drawers are cleaned out, as is the refrigerator and freezer.

HEKSHERS

Before industrialization, when all food was fresh and not packaged or processed, one did not necessarily need to worry about the kashrut of specific foods. However, now that so many foods are packaged and processed one must check for a specific mark on the packaging of the food to verify that it is kosher. This mark, referred to as a *heksher* or a *teudah*, is on a visible area of the packaging and is actually a trademarked sign in the United States.

There are countless different types of *hekshers* that one may find on foods, anything from potato chips to canned peaches to dried pasta. All areas of food have at least one brand that has a *heksher*. There are some Jewish Americans who keep kosher in their home who rely completely on the *heksher* to let them know about the kashrut of certain foods. There are others, however, who are satisfied to examine the list of ingredients and determine from that whether or not a product is kosher.

Some extremely observant Jewish Americans require that all produce, milk, soap, sponges, water, and other dairy products also have a *heksher*. Water and produce are required to be marked as kosher because there is a fear of bugs or other insects, and soap and sponges are required to be marked because they come into direct contact with the food and could have, at some time in production, come into contact with nonkosher ingredients. Many soaps, for example, are made from animal fats.

ETHICAL KASHRUT

Since the beginnings of kashrut there have always been questions about cruelty to animals and other ethical issues involved in kashrut. American Jews particularly have been concerned with ethical kashrut since the countercultural movement of the 1960s. It is only natural that Jews be concerned over the ethics of kashrut, because the entire system of laws is based completely on preventing cruelty to animals and promoting good health. Although in the past there have been some critics of kashrut who have attacked the method of slaughter, the way in which kosher animals are killed has proven to be the most humane method of slaughter.

Starting in the 1970s there were questions not about the slaughtering itself, but about the method of preparing the animal for slaughter, which is called hoisting and shackling. Although the sight of hoisting and shackling is quite disturbing, the degree of pain is exaggerated by appearance. However, there are special pens that have been developed that put the animal into position for slaughter with less pain or discomfort.

There has also been a question for many years about the possibility of stunning the animal with either electricity or anesthesia before it is slaughtered; however, most rabbis have ruled that this would be contrary to the laws of kashrut.

Most recently, questions have been raised not about the treatment of the animals in kosher slaughterhouses, but about the treatment of the workers. When it was found that the world's largest kosher meatpacking plant, located in Iowa, was mistreating its workers by giving insufficient pay and having questionable safety measures and abusive supervisors, many rabbis were outraged. Since that time, leaders of the Conservative movement are planning to create a new ethical certification system. The new *heksher* will signify that kosher food producers have met a set of standards that determine the social responsibility of kosher food producers, particularly in the area of workers' rights. The group working on this will not use this *heksher* as a replacement for others; rather, meat that has been okayed will get two separate *hekshers*.

Individual Adaptations to Kashrut

The laws of kashrut are varied and complex. While they are followed to the letter by some American Jews, others follow the spirit but not the letter of the law—for example, avoiding pork, shellfish, and combining meat and milk but substituting boiling water for a *mikveh* for new utensils or allowing nonkosher wine during everyday meals. Still other Jewish Americans do not keep kosher homes but cook kosher-style meals for Jewish holidays, while others ignore the laws completely.

Health

While many American Jews and non-Jews alike associate a kosher diet with health and safe food, there is really little basis for this. Food that is kosher can still cause food-borne illness just like nonkosher food. One can eat a very healthy kosher meal full of whole grains and fresh fruits and vegetables. Or one can eat a very unhealthy kosher meal full of refined sugars and fats.

Many traditional Jewish foods, especially from the Ashkenazi diet, are full of nutritional red flags: few fresh fruits and vegetables, low in fiber, high in fat, high in refined flours and sugars. Of course, such foods may be delicious.

There is a good deal of medical research that shows that Ashkenazi Jews actually have higher rates of irritable bowel syndrome, Crohn's disease, and ulcerative colitis. The rate of Ashkenazi Jews in America with these diseases is even higher, because they commonly occur in northern industrialized countries. Generally these conditions can be controlled by monitoring one's diet.

In terms of other health and nutrition issues among Jewish Americans it is common to find many polarities in the nutritional status of people, even in individual families. The traditional Jewish foods that are loaded with red meat and heavy dairy products and are devoid of vitamin-rich vegetables are giving way to more health-conscious preparations and styles of cooking. As the vegetarian and health food industry is growing, so too is the Jewish American health craze growing.

As Americans in general contend with overweight and obesity and other health problems such as diabetes and heart disease, so too are Jewish Americans looking to create healthier lifestyles. There are a lot of efforts to make traditional Jewish fare healthier. For example, food companies and community groups are promoting healthier versions of Jewish recipes. A noodle kugel usually made with cream cheese, eggs, and sugar can be made with low-fat cream cheese, yolk-free noodles, and reduced sugar. In addition there is an effort to introduce healthy foods from other cultures into the Jewish American diet. Kosher sushi, for example, has become a popular Sunday evening meal in some Jewish neighborhoods in the United States.

NOTES

1. Kosherfest: The Business of Kosher Food and Beverage, http://Kosherfest.com.

2. Marvin Harris, *Good to Eat: Riddles of Food and Culture* (New York: Simon and Schuster, 1985).

3. Mary Douglas, *Purity and Danger* (London: Routledge, 1966).

4. Rabbi Isaac Klein, cited in Rabbinical Assembly (January 2007), http://rabbinicalassembly.org.

Glossary

Ashkenazi   Jews mostly from Eastern Europe and Germanic countries.

bar mitzvah   ceremony where 13-year-old boy enters into Jewish adulthood.

bat mitzvah   ceremony where 12- or 13-year-old girl enters into Jewish adulthood.

birkat hamazon   prayer of thanks for after a meal that can be found in almost all prayer books and is often printed in a variety of artistic styles in a small booklet called a *birchon*.

blech   any hotplate, warming drawer, or stovetop cover that is used to keep foods warm.

bris   naming ceremony for infant male including circumcision.

challah   generally a round or braided bread enriched with eggs prepared specifically for the Sabbath but eaten on the Sabbath and any other time.

chametz   leaven.

cholent   thick beef, barley, and bean porridge.

cholev yisroel   specific **kosher** symbol for dairy foods.

etrog   citrus fruit used on **Sukkot.**

Hanukkah   festival of lights; a Talmudic holiday marking the miraculous victory of the Jews, led by the Maccabees, against Greek persecution and religious oppression.

kasha   buckwheat.

kasher   to purify and bless (usually a kitchen or utensil) making it kosher.

kashrut   Jewish dietary laws.

Kiddish   blessing over wine or grape juice recited at Shabbat and holiday meals. May also refer to the small snack or spread of food after Jewish services or celebrations at a synagogue.

kippa   yarmulke or head covering.

kosher   following the Jewish dietary laws or *kashrut*.

lox   cured salmon.

lulav   palm branch used on **Sukkot.**

mashgiach   special type of rabbi or trained rabbinical appointee who checks that the kitchen and dining areas of restaurants uphold the laws of **kashrut.** A *mashgiach tamidit* is at the restaurant all the time. A *mashgiach nichnas v'yotzei* visits factories a few times a year.

matzah   unleavened bread.

Mishnah   third-century rabbinic text consisting of six books of religious and civil laws.

Orthodox Union (OU)   an association that certifies kosher food products and supervises kosher kitchens.

pareve   neither meat nor dairy.

Passover (Pesach)   holiday whose rituals are taken from the **Torah.** The primary observances are related to the Exodus from Egypt after generations of slavery.

Passover seder   service taken from the Mishnah and observed before Pesach dinner, recounting the Exodus from Egypt.

Purim   Talmudic holiday that celebrates a historic Jewish victory over enemies.

Rosh Hashana   high holy day, Head of the Year, the Jewish New Year.

schmaltz   rendered chicken fat.

seder   literally means "order" in Hebrew and describes any service or sequence of actions that take place before a meal.

Sephardi   Jews living in or from throughout the Mediterranean, Iberia, North Africa, and the Middle East.

Shabbat   Sabbath; Jewish day of rest observed each week from one hour before sundown on Friday until sundown on Saturday.

Shavuot   last of three pilgrimage harvests; celebrates the time in which God gave the **Torah** to the Jewish people.

shtetls   small, confined, and crowded religious Jewish communities in Eastern Europe.

Simchat Torah   "Rejoicing in the Torah." Holiday marking the completion of the annual cycle of weekly Torah readings.

Sukkot   pilgrimage harvest festival commemorating the 40-year period during which the Israelites were wandering in the desert, living in temporary shelters.

Talmud   book of oral law, which includes Rabbinic expansion, explanation, and argument on the Mishnah.

Tanach   Jewish Bible, which includes the Torah, the Book of Prophets, and the Writings.

Torah   first five books of the Bible, including Genesis, Exodus, Leviticus, Numbers, and Deuteronomy. Torahs are in scroll form and are read publicly in the synagogue on Shabbat, holidays, and some weekdays.

treyf   nonkosher.

tzimmes   sweet carrot and raisin dish traditionally served on **Rosh Hashanah.**

Yiddish   Hebrew/German dialect spoken by **Ashekanazi** Jews.

Yom Kippur   high holy day, fast day, most important and introspective holiday of the Jewish calendar.

Resource Guide

Online and print resources have been extremely helpful in preparing this book. Although there are few introductory references devoted to Jewish American food culture as this one is, there is a wealth of material on Jewish food and dietary laws, Judaism, and Jewish life, Jewish American history and culture, and social and cultural aspects of food that informed this volume—and can further inform the reader.

COOKBOOKS

Cookbooks are a great source of learning, not only how to prepare the food of a culture but also what sort of foods are eaten in everyday life and for various events, and how they came to be. Many Jewish and Jewish American cookbooks also contain rich histories and cultural documentation. A recipe can be a story in itself. Community cookbooks, usually compilations of the home recipes of women in a community, are also great tools for cultural and historical research. Joan Nathan, the maven of Jewish American cooking, has a number of books—*Jewish Cooking in America* (New York: Knopf, 1995) and *The Jewish Holiday Kitchen* (New York: Schocken, 1998) are especially valuable. For young readers she also wrote *The Children's Jewish Holiday Kitchen* (New York: Schocken, 2000). Claudia Roden's *The Book of Jewish Food: An Odyssey from Samarkand to New York* (New York: Knopf, 1996) tells a history of the Jewish Diaspora through its food and recipes. Also important are Joyce Goldstein's *Sephardic Flavors* (San Francisco: Chronicle Books, 2000) and *The Essential Book of Jewish Festival Cooking* (New York: William Morrow

Cookbooks, 2004) by Phyllis and Miriyam Glazer. Finally, Mitchell Davis's *The Mensch Chef* (New York: Clarkson Potter, 2004) humorously introduces readers to Ashkenazi Jewish standards and some updated versions of the classics.

CULTURAL STUDIES OF FOOD

There are other Jewish food books that contain recipes; however, they are not cookbooks but are rather historical or cultural studies of food and culture. David Kraemer's *Jewish Eating and Identity through the Ages* (New York: Routledge, 2007), which considers social aspects of Jews and food from biblical times to the present day, manages both. So does Marcie Cohen Ferris, in *Matzoh Ball Gumbo: Culinary Tales of the Jewish South* (Chapel Hill: University of North Carolina Press, 2005), a history and journey through Jewish food and culture of the American South. While not focused on the American Jewish experience but rather Jews in general, John Cooper's *Eat and be Satisfied: A Social History of Jewish Food* (Lanham, MD: Jason Aronson, 1994) and Oded Schwartz's *In Search of Plenty: A History of Jewish Food* (North Pomfret, VT: Trafalgar Square, 1993) explore Jewish food history from biblical times to the present. The edited volume *Food and Judaism* (Omaha, NE: Creighton University Press, 2005) focuses less on history and more on culture, much of it American. More specific to the American Jewish immigrant experience is Hasia Diner's *Hungering for America* (Cambridge, MA: Harvard University Press, 2002), which juxtaposes the American immigrant foodways of the Irish, Italians, and Jews. Finally, because of New York's important role as a U.S. immigration hub for Jews as well as so many cultures, Annie Hauck-Lawson and Jonathan Deutsch's edited volume *Gastropolis: New York at Table* (New York: Columbia University Press, 2008) contains some important chapters such as those by Suzanne Wasserman on pushcart peddlers, Mark Russ Federman on his family business "Russ and Daughters," and Jennifer Berg on the many New York iconic foods (bagels and lox, knish, cheesecake) that are Jewish in origin.

DIETARY LAW

Jewish dietary law is its own genre of Jewish food books. Resources in this area generally fall into one of two categories: guides to the correct practice of kashrut and interpretations of the law, often written by rabbis, and. books *about* kashrut, specifically how these complicated and proscriptive laws came to be and how they have endured. *The Practical Guide to Kashrus* by Rabbi Shaul Wagschal (Brooklyn, NY: Judaica Press, 1991) is a standard example of the first type. Lise Stern's *How to Keep Kosher: A Comprehensive Guide to*

Understanding Jewish Dietary Laws (New York: William Morrow Cookbooks, 2004) is more accessible to non-Jews. In the second category of books about the origins and cultural roles of dietary laws, Marvin Harris's *The Sacred Cow and the Abominable Pig: Riddles of Food and Culture* (New York: Touchstone Books, 1987), Mary Douglas's *Purity and Danger: An Analysis of the Concepts of Pollution and Taboo* (New York: Routledge, 2002), and Jean Soler's *The Dietary Prohibitions of the Hebrews* (New York: The New York Review, 1979) are classic works on this topic, each with very different perspectives and theories. Newer contributions are Frederick Simoons's *Eat Not This Flesh: Food Avoidances from Prehistory to the Present* (Madison: University of Wisconsin Press, 1994) and Gillian Feely-Harnik's *The Lord's Table: The Meaning of Food in Early Judaism and Christianity* (Washington, DC: Smithsonian Institution Press, 1994).

JEWISH AMERICAN CULTURE

There are a plethora of sources on Jews and Jewish American life that, although not food-focused per se, can provide historical and cultural insight into the Jewish people. The most comprehensive of these is the 22-volume *Encyclopedia Judaica* (New York: Macmillan, 2006), which does include some food entries. *The Jew in the Modern World: A Documentary History* (New York: Oxford University Press, 1995) edited by Paul Mendes-Flohr and Jehuda Reinharz, is a useful source on Jewry in general, while *The American Jewish Experience* (Teaneck, NJ: Holmes & Meier Publishers, 1997) edited by Jonathan Sarna, *The Jew in the American World* (Detroit, MI: Wayne State University Press, 1996), edited by Jacob Rader Marcus, and Chaim Waxman's *America's Jews in Transition* (Philadelphia: Temple University Press, 1983) are go-to sources on American Jewish life, both past and present.

Finally, there are sources that contribute to our understanding of the complex and intimate connection between people and their food. Carole Counihan and Penny Van Esterik's *Food and Culture: A Reader* (New York: Routledge, 2008) and Counihan's *Food in the US* (New York: Routledge, 2002) are good places to start in learning about how scholars have considered this connection. For American history, consider Harvey Levenstein's *Revolution at the Table: The Transformation of the American Diet* (Berkeley: University of California Press, 2003) and Donna Gabaccia's *We Are What We Eat: Ethnic Food and the Making of Americans* (Cambridge, MA: Harvard University Press, 2000). For reference, James Trager's *The Food Chronology: A Food Lover's Compendium of Events and Anecdotes, from Prehistory to the Present* (New York: Owl Books, 1997) provides fun facts about the history of food.

WEB SITES

Jewish and Jewish American recipes abound online with both formal sites and informal discussion groups devoted to the topic. Some are religious in nature, focusing on cooking within the laws of kashrut, while others focus on cultural aspects of Jewish food. Some recommended sites are:

Jewish Recipes (http://jewishrecipes.org). Features information about traditional foods as well as recipes.

Classic Jewish Food Recipe Archives (http://jewish-food.org). A huge collection of recipes, many submitted by users.

Beyond food and cooking, the Library of Congress's "From Haven to Home: 350 Years of Jewish Life in America" (http://www.loc.gov/exhibits/haventohome/timeline/haven-timeline_index.html) provides an interactive overview of the history of American Jewry. Another good resource is "Jews in America: Our Story" from the Center for Jewish History (http://www.jewsinamerica.org).

For general work on food and culture and food history, Lynne Oliver's encyclopedic timeline and resource guide, "The Food Timeline" (http://www.foodtimeline.org) is a good place to start. Another wonderful resource for food studies is the University of Michigan's "Feeding America: The Historic American Cookbook Project," a digital cookbook collection that includes some historically important cookbooks including many Jewish American titles (http://digital.lib.msu.edu/projects/cookbooks/index.html).

Some Jewish American organizations and institutions are also good resources for food information. The National Museum of American Jewish History in Philadelphia gives a lot of attention to Jewish American food (http://www.nmajh.org) and has examples of Jewish American food artifacts on its Web site. The Orthodox Union, widely known for its kosher certifications, provides a wealth of information on kashrut available through its Web site (http://oukosher.org/).

Selected Bibliography

Cooper, John. *Eat and Be Satisfied: A Social History of Jewish Food.* Lanham, MD: Rowman and Littlefield, 1993.

Curtin, Deane W., and Lisa M. Heldke, eds. *Cooking, Eating, Thinking: Transformative Philosophies of Food.* Bloomington: Indiana University Press, 1992.

Douglas, Mary. *Purity and Danger.* London: Routledge, 1966.

Farber, Roberta Rosenberg, and Chaim I. Waxman, eds. *Jews in America: A Contemporary Reader.* Waltham, MA: Brandeis University Press, 1999.

Feeley-Harnik, Gillian. *The Lord's Table: The Meaning of Food in Early Judaism and Christianity.* Washington, DC: Smithsonian Institution Press, 1994.

Glazer, Nathan. *American Judaism.* 2nd ed. Chicago: University of Chicago Press, 1989.

Glazer, Phyllis, and Miriyam Glazer. *The Essential book of Jewish Festival Cooking.* New York: Harper Collins, 2004.

Goldstein, Joyce. *Sephardic Flavors.* San Francisco: Chronicle Books, 2000.

Greenspoon, Leonard J., Ronald A. Simkins, and Gerrald Shapiro, eds. *Food and Judaism.* Omaha, NE: Creighton University Press, 1995.

Harris, Marvin. *Good to Eat: Riddles of Food and Culture.* New York: Simon and Schuster, 1985.

Klein, Isaac. *A Jewish Guide to Religious Practice.* New York: The Jewish Theological Seminary of America, 1992.

Marcus, Jacob Rader, ed. *The Jew in the American World.* Detroit, MI: Wayne State University Press, 1997.

Mendes-Flohr, Paul, and Jehuda Reinharz, eds. *The Jew in the Modern World: A Documentary History.* 2nd ed. New York: Oxford University Press, 1995.

Nathan, Joan. *Jewish Cooking in America.* New York: Knopf, 1995.

———. *Jewish Holiday Cookbook.* New York: Shocken, 2005.

Pritchard, James B., ed. *The Ancient Near East*. Vol. 1. Princeton, NJ: Princeton University Press, 1973.

Sarna, Jonathan D., ed. *The American Jewish Experience*. 2nd ed. New York: Holmes and Meier, 1997.

Schwartz, Oded. *In Search of Plenty: A History of Jewish Food*. Toronto: Culture Concepts, 1992.

Shanks, Hershel, ed. *Ancient Israel: From Abraham to the Roman Destruction of the Temple*. Englewood Cliffs, NJ: Prentice-Hall, 1999.

Simoons, Frederick J. *Eat Not This Flesh: Food Avoidances from Prehistory to the Present*. 2nd ed. Madison: University of Wisconsin Press, 1994.

Wagshal, Shaul. *The Practical Guide to Kashrus*. Brooklyn, NY: Judaica Press, 1991.

Waxman, Chaim I. *America's Jews in Transition*. Philadelphia: Temple University Press, 1983.

Index

About the Authors

JONATHAN DEUTSCH is Assistant Professor of Tourism and Hospitality and Director of the Culinary Management Center, Kingsborough Community College, City University of New York, Secretary of the Association for the Study of Food and Society, and co-editor of *Gastropolis: Food and New York City* (2008).

RACHEL D. SAKS is a graduate student in Nutrition and Dietetics at New York University. She has attended various culinary schools.